EXACTING CLAM No. 9 — Summer 2023

I0641225

CONTENTS

Front cover: "The Better to See You With" by Royce M. Becker

Quintagrams in black boxes by Richard Kostelanetz

© 2023 Sagging Meniscus Press
All Rights Reserved

ISBN: 978-1-952386-69-5

exactingclam.com

Exacting Clam is a quarterly publication from Sagging Meniscus.

Contributing Editors: Jake Goldsmith, Kurt Luchs, Melissa McCarthy, M.J. Nicholls, Thomas Walton
House Metaclamician: Christopher Boucher
Senior Editors: Jeff Chon, Elizabeth Cooperman, Tyler C. Gore, Doug Nufer
Fiction Editor: Charles Holdefer
Poetry Editor: Aaron Anstett
Reviews Editor: Jesi Bender
Executive Editor: Guillermo Stitch
Publisher: Jacob Smullyan

From the Editor

I can't believe I catched this on video. Attend to me. They will enter your life who are meant only to be there for a time. These are insignificant vestiges. They are as testicles. You are the penis. Wink at a penis, it rises, but *oh* how heavy the balls. Don't think twice about detaching them. Their forays are few. Some testicles hang too low even to swing. *You won't believe it either.* Listen. We are coming for you. Our business won't take long. We do not want peace. We are not friends. We are suckerfish. You are belly. Behold! The belly breaches but not the fish. Take not fright ye. We are prodigious—in our number only the finless go down. *When you see it.* Do please remember on your way out, ladies & gents, that this is a residential area. I shouldn't talk but. She goes for a certain type bless her. Transients. Rag and bone. She is the economy. She overheats, banks topple. And who can blame them? *You won't be able to unsee it.* If this were engraved with needles in the corner of the eye, it would serve as a lesson to the heedful. In the wadi you will find the digital nomads. They are credulous. You will be as a god to them. They will quake. You will gain three centimetres in height. They will quail. Leave them to their nomading. They would only burn on cresting the ridge. Don't fear. They have not forgotten you but await your return. *Watch till the end.* Warning. Use gloves.

Prolonged contact may cause harm. Ingredients include Sodium Xylenesulfonate, Denatonium Benzoate and Hydroxypropyltrimonium. Active agent is 6-(2-Aminopropyl)benzofuran, a serotonin–norepinephrine–dopamine reuptake inhibitor. Effects include disinhibition and novelty enhancement. Some ions never get around to forming molecules. Neither 5-Methoxy-N,N-diisopropyltryptamine, 4-Acetoxy-N,N- nor 3,4-Methylenedioxypyrovalerone are substituted piperazines. One Arylcyclohexylamine is much the same as the next. *I had to watch ten times.* Gather round. We can win this. Jesionowski, I'm going to need you to go ahead and track back when we're defending. You're not actually meant to loll about in the box all the time, you *fucking diva*. These guys are working hard for you. When and only when we have possession, that's when you make your fancy little runs. Karpowicz, Augspurger and Ó Súilleabháin—hold your positions. You're not offensive. If I see you out wide again, Beaufoy, you're benched. We all of us must allow Jesionowski to soar. This it seems is our destiny. *Wait for it.* Attention please. Would passenger Hephzibah Rafferty please make your way to Gate 41A. Your flight closes in ten minutes and we are worried about you. Not angry, to be clear. We're aware of Skybender®, the state-of-the-art retail experience in whose polished surfaces you have doubtless paused here and there to see your reflection. We recognise its gleaming qualities, the sirens that call to you from its attractively lit display areas, the merfolk that swim the channels between its *chanels*. We get it. But your plane is leaving. Bid adieu to the fawning attendants—they cannot come with you. You, and you alone, and the other passengers on the aircraft, await the miracle of flight. Think of it! To go up into the very *sky*? Like a goddess? And watch a movie up there? A *current release?* What can the earthbound know of Heaven's delights? Today you fly to Denver, but Denver is just an *idea* to them, Hephzibah. Lindette, who was so good at picking out those top notes you like—bergamot, cardamom—is aerophobic. She works here on the advice of her exposure therapist. *Wait for it . . .* Stop.

Authorised personnel only beyond this point. Oh, is that you, Hector? Well, *come on in*, ya silly billy! We didn't realize it was you or we wouldn't have . . . wait. Sydney isn't with you, is he? Felix? Thick as thieves you three. If Sydney and/or Felix are with you we have a problem. Sydney and Felix are unauthorised personnel. As you well know. The temerity, actually, that you imagined you could just stroll beyond this point with Sydney and/or Felix. It's a little disappointing. We couldn't have been clearer on this when we authorised you. Unauthorised personnel are bad people, Hector. *Terrible* people. Especially Felix—a man in whom all the vices are united. *Wait . . .*

Connie Woodring

The Poem Is Mightier Than the Sword

Despicable atrocities.
Horrendous.
Disquieting and dispiriting.
Outrageous.
Horrifying torture.
Unending suffering.
Genocide and tyranny.
No words to describe it.
Inhumane.
Barbarous.
Fiendish.
Catastrophic.
Diabolical.
Beyond comprehension.
Hell on earth.

If this poem is published, it will end all wars.

Melissa McCarthy

Wobbly Photography

. . . regularly through last year the Zoom-enabled Glue Factory took monthly consignment of a roving report on whatever topic—usually related to war, sharks, and literature—was top of my mind. Here's the news from September, on some unexpected photographic connections.

Hello.

I've been working on early photography, learning about the methods and substances used by the Victorian pioneers.

Techniques in the 1850s included the photogenic drawing on salted paper and the calotype; the daguerreotype, on silver-plated copper; and the wet collodion process, using glass plates to make negatives.

It's notable that many of these photographic trailblazers made much more use of stuff, of unprocessed things that we would still recognize as substances: Sir John Herschel, for example, used the acid from oak galls, a fungus growing on the trees in his stately grounds. Or eggs—at the height of photomania, and to my delight, albumen from egg whites was in such demand, for treating the photographic paper, that six million eggs a year were used in Britain, just for this. There were "girls [who] did nothing else all day but break eggs and separate the whites from the yolks," (says curator D. B. Thomas), and it was a seasonal business: they produced more photographic paper, and more images, at the times of year when hens were laying more prolifically.

But we've moved on, in photography. Past the wet plates and the eggs, past silver halide, explosive nitrate, celluloid, to the digital. (Though I think the filmmaker David Cronenberg harks back to Victorian photography, preoccupied as he is with the interface between the messy, wet human body, and transmission of the image.) I'm still interested in the old stuff, however, and I've become fascinated by a particular substrate of images, which is: the damp or the wobbly photograph. I'm interested in there being something not quite solid in the photographic image.

I'll tell you about a couple of cases of this odd photography.

First, there is the British writer Rebecca West, in her book *Black Lamb and Grey Falcon*, which is, as in the subtitle, *the record of a journey through Yugoslavia in 1937.*

This is a hugely underappreciated book, in which West, in the company of a Jewish Serb poet-administrator-guide, a taciturn chauffeur named Dragutin, and her husband, who over the course of twelve hundred pages is only ever named as "my husband," travels all over Yugoslavia learning about its history over two millennia, about the landscape, buildings, and peoples: ßabout the current political state of play.

She's a very funny writer—she describes arriving at an inn run by an "awe-inspiring landlady. She was one of those widows whose majesty makes their husbands seem specially dead."—but it's a terrifying book, because of her awareness of the cataclysm that's about to descend. West gives a stunning account, heard from one of her contacts, of the assassination of Franz Ferdinand. Then she imagines the Archduke, a dementedly fanatical game hunter, in the reception hall of the palace at Sarajevo, where hordes of taxidermied animals line the walls: "Their animal eyes, clear and dark as water, would brightly watch the approach of their slayer to an end that exactly resembled their own."

And the dedication, when the book is published in 1941, is:

> "To my friends in Yugoslavia
> Who are now all dead or enslaved"

With her emphasis on Yugoslavia as the frontline where the Muslim invasion of Europe was repulsed to preserve Christendom, she'd be considered now as racist, snobbish, imperialist, obsessed with blood and purity. But it's a fascinating book.

To concentrate here just on the photography aspect, this is her description of Lake Scutari (abridged slightly):

> a few more turns of the road took us to a view of Lake Scutari; and indeed it was among landscapes what dragons are among beasts. Through a deep fiord, a thousand feet or so below us, a river flowed into the lake, slowly and without confusion of the two substances, as water from a dripping tap might seep into a cask of molasses. For this lake is not water, it is mud. It was green as a horse-pond on an English common, but the substance was not so liquid. It was nearly solid; the reflections it bears were not su-

perficial images which a breeze will confuse and annul, but photographs imposed on a sensitive jelly.

> [The reflections on it were] more solid, more dogged, more of a fact than reflections commonly are, because they were registered on this viscid medium. [. . .] In this landscape there had happened to matter what happens to time when, as they say, it stands still. Mobility was not.

> Here nature was at its most unnatural: and the scale of the scene, which was immense, as much as the eye could see from a great height, made this prodigiousness alarming. It was as if one learned that nightmares might fill not only a troubled house after midnight but the whole of the night and the day, that a historical epoch might hold horror and nothing else. Yet it was beautiful, so beautiful that the appalled sight could not have enough of it.

She's, as you can hear, describing this lake that seems to retain reflections in it like a jelly holding a photographic image, and she's commenting on the impending dread this inspires.

That's Rebecca West, published in 1941, noticing strange photography in the landscape that's about to collapse again into one war. And another . . .

Then I noticed a second example of this strange, not-quite-liquid photography. You might protest that what I'm about to describe is not photography, not quite. But. Come with me through the water meadows, woods, and gardens of seventeenth-century Yorkshire, and we'll see. I am proposing another example of a long, weird, war-torn, panoramic landscape description. It's Andrew Marvell's *Upon Appleton House*, which was first printed in the Folio of 1681, three years after his death. (Discussion can ensue about whether to say his name MAR-vl or mar-VELL.)

Upon Appleton House is quite the psychedelic mash-up of genre, argument, and imagery. It's a history of the eponymous building and the family who own it. It's a paean to the beauty and virtue of Lord Fairfax's daughter Mary. At its kernel there is a lament about the fact that there has just been an actual civil war (from 1642 to 1651), rather than just a plant-based simulacrum of battle and military order. The poem is a landscape appreciation. It's architectural criticism. It's an exercise in classical Latin style. It's an experiment in multiple fashions of describing the countryside, with expansively odd and quick-changing imagery and metaphor.

My favourite example of this is where one of the evil lesbian nuns who used to inhabit Appleton House compares herself and her fellow sisters to crystallized fruits: their piety, she attempts to persuade an heiress, is the preserving sugar that stops their pleasurable flesh from rotting. My critical response to this is, *What?*

But, the main reason the poem hooked my attention is nearer to the end, when the narrator describes an idyllic English country evening, through which the heroine Maria is walking, making the garden beautiful as she goes. And just before she's described, there's an element of comparison. Maria is the second half of a pair, following on from a prior creature who also stills the evening. And

that matching part, the first term of the two, is a kingfisher.

The poem reads (in two stanzas):

So when the shadows laid asleep
From underneath these banks do creep,
And on the river as it flows
With eben shuts begin to close;
The modest halcyon comes in sight,
Flying betwixt the day and night;
And such an horror calm and dumb,
Admiring Nature does benumb.

The viscous air, wheres'e'er she fly,
Follows and sucks her azure dye;
The jellying stream compacts below,
If it might fix her shadow so;
The stupid fishes hang, as plain
As flies in crystal overta'en;
And men the silent scene assist,
Charmed with the sapphire-winged mist.

The narrator is describing how a kingfisher or halcyon flies over the water and transforms all its substance and its light; somehow the viscous air osmoses into blue, the jellying stream tries to retain the bird's shadow, tries to hold the image. The water crystallizes with fish in, and the whole scene is full of sapphire-winged mist. This is brilliant, and, to my mind, it's hugely photographic, with the surface, the crystals, the jelly retaining the image of what has passed over and been preserved by an action of the light.

And it's also very like Rebecca West's description of Lake Scutari, which holds the reflections, the pictures, in its gelatinous, not really liquid, not quite solid surface.

They're both—Andrew Marvell and Rebecca West—providing examples of a sort of wobbly photography, a damp receiving surface that holds an image though it's not quite steady.

There's a third example of this unstable photography that came to me, which appears in Chris Marker's 1962 film *La Jetée*, which is made up of a sequence of still images, all still black and white photos, except for one, when the hero's girlfriend suddenly moves, moves her photographic head to look at him. The photo wasn't still nor a photo, really, after all, and again it's in the context of a story of shadowy, time-travelling, global war.

I haven't fixed or clarified what to make of all of this viscous photography; this is a preliminary report, still to be developed, crystallized. I'm just reporting, for now, on an odd phenomenon: this appearance of unstable pictures, and a fear of war.

I'll leave you to consider the picture under your own lights, see what image stabilises on your surfaces, what sticks with you.

Thanks.

James Sallis

Zora Neale Hurston and Langston Hughes Drive Through the South

Houses career crazily in their utter desertion
as Zora and Langston cruise at 20 miles an hour
in her Nash two-seater through the slow South.
Towns fall away, Richmond, Tuskegee, Mobile,
drawling up into the sky left behind.
Zora has a gun in a shoulder holster, Langston
has a notebook. On the old Atlantic Highway,
renamed US 1, she pushes the little coupe hard
and lands a speeding ticket.

Biscuits, ham, cornbread, watermelon,
Langston writes down meals in his notebook.
They ask what songs people know, visit
with conjure and college men. Photos show
Zora in white dress and beads, Langston
with his tie loosened, the Nash waiting nearby,
thinking how it will be a get-away car
when it grows up. None of the three suspect
they'll be running these roads till they end.

THOMAS WALTON

UNSAVORY THOUGHTS

WHAT'S IN A SWAN?

I am in a poetry group. A kind of book group, but we only read poems. I know, don't worry, this will be short.

Our poem was Marianne Moore's poem, "No Swan So Fine," about the swan that's carved into the sculpture—"at ease and tall? the king is dead"—from the Viking edition of her *Complete Poems*. There's a note that says it is the author's "final revision."

We were sitting in the park. Behind the museum. The bugs were out. We were swatting them as we discussed the unfortunate blind spots in the current political landscape. How the far Right sees only the far Left's intolerance, and not its own. And how the far Left sees only the far Right's intolerance, and not its own.

When she opened the book and read the poem, we fell silent. The poem had no concern for the materialism of politics, that much was evident. The poem was not interested in participating in any willing myopia or reductive thinking such as is required to think in political terms. The poem, "No Swan So Fine," wasn't even about a swan!

A stone, I suppose, in the shape of a swan. Kevin thought it was part of the fountain from the opening quote. But Allie said "something like a candelabrum." And Sven just said, dumbly, "swan," merely recognizing the word but unable to follow its movement as it glided slowly through the poem, refusing to reveal itself as stone, statue, fountain or fall. I suppose it was a phantom.

"Perhaps it's all of these," said the one who had read it aloud, and we all groaned.

"What?" she asked.

"You can't just zoom out like that." said Allie.

"Why not?"

"I don't know . . . it's too cliché."

"Yeah, it's cliché," repeated Sven, the one who'd earlier said "swan."

"It's too vague," said Kevin, "we want answers!"

"Good luck with that."

"It's stone, okay. It's obviously stone. And besides, who cares? You miss the point. It's not a fucking mystery novel . . ." Jordan said, with a little too much anger for a poetry club.

There was an awkward silence. Someone slapped a bug. A dog ran by, chasing a ball, then ran back with the ball in its mouth.

"Fucking DeSantis," someone said, and then started talking (again) about the inability of the "human animal" to see its own flaws.

I asked which was the animal that could, but was unanimously ignored.

YOU'RE NEVER TOO YOUNG TO GET DEMENTIA

"You should write about it."

"What?"

"I just think it's so crazy."

"Oh, that . . . yeah."

"It would be easy to do."

We were in the kitchen. She was sitting at the bar. We called it the bar, but it was just a high table someone left in one of the apartments after they moved out. I brought it home. She didn't want it at first, but then we started calling it the bar and now we use it all the time.

I set a gin and soda in front of her. On the bar.

"You never see things like that anymore," she said.

"No. It's true."

"Not here anyway."

"Not anywhere."

"Not anymore. It's extraordinary," she said, and sipped her drink.

I got up and pulled the bottle out of the freezer. The kitchen was small. The apartment was small. Not New York small, but small. The kitchen was very small. The fridge was just right there by the bar, and on the other side of it was the stove. I stood up, turned, opened the freezer, pulled out the bottle, turned again, and poured some gin in my glass. I left the bottle on the table. She poured me a splash of soda from the can that was already out.

"That's plenty."

"Sorry."

"It's okay. I can't believe I forgot the limes," I said.

"Ella's friend has dementia."

"I don't have dementia," I said. "And besides, they're old."

"They're in their sixties."

"Well, that's old."

"Not to get dementia."

"No. I guess you're right. It's young to get dementia."

"You forgot the limes last time, too."

"Very funny . . ."

"Well you did," she said, and raised her eyebrows.

"I've always forgotten things. I used to go to school without my backpack all the time. My mother would have to drop it off for me."

"That's different."

"Can we change the subject? Want another drink?"

"Not yet," she said. "Ella said she'll be eating dinner and then, five minutes later, ask when it'll be time for dinner. And she'll actually eat a whole other plate of food. Ella says she's getting . . . well, she's gained a lot of weight."

"Weird."

"She said zaftig."

"She said zaftig what?"

"Zaftig like her friend is getting zaftig."

"Zaftig. What is that? Hebrew?"

"Yiddish."

"Yiddish."

"Yiddish, it means fat. Not fat, really. More like plump. Full-figured."

"Uh huh," I said, and stood up, turned, grabbed some ice out of the freezer and put it in my glass. I turned again and sat down, filled my glass. She picked up the soda can . . . "No thanks," I said.

"I'll have one more, I guess."

I poured the gin into her glass, then stood up. "Where are the limes?" I said, looking in the fridge.

"Funny," she said.

I sat back down at the bar. The sun was coming in through the window. It was hot. The cold gin and sodas were a relief. I was trying to remember when she moved into this place. It had already been a few years.

"Do you think I'm zaftig?" she said, and stood up.

"No," I said, "you're fat."

She hit my shoulder. "Anyway, you should write about it. It would be easy."

"Why don't *you* write about it?"

"Maybe I will . . . you never see things like that anymore."

"No, it's true . . . you don't."

How 'bout Another Phillip Lopate Anthology

Certain gestures in contemporary essay writing drive me crazy. You know the ones. Those committed on a regular, recurring basis. As if they've become part of the form itself. I suppose they've become part of the form itself. The profound-personal-experience-relating-to-the-subject gesture, for instance, is abominable. As is the humorous-anecdote-placed-ever-so-cleverly gesture. I can't stand it! It's never more humorous than it is predictable.

By far my least favorite gesture in contemporary essay writing (and the most *a la mode*) is what amounts to a weird kind of name-dropping. You're reading the essay, and then suddenly there's a quote from a famous scholar, a celebrated writer, a fashionable intellectual or (very clever!) an unexpectedly low-brow pop star or athlete. These formal tropes are nauseating. How long will we continue with them?

In *Me and Other Writings*, Marguerite Duras says this about her work: "What I write makes me want to die, it's only natural that it makes others want to die too."

There you see? I just committed the name-dropping gesture. Isn't it horrid? Isn't it putrid and expected? Like a bowel movement in the morning. Did you hear how contrived it was? Whenever I come across someone quoting Wittgenstein or Pascal (both in fashion in this century) all I can think is "I wish I was reading Wittgenstein or Pascal instead of this essay."

I admit that reading contemporary essays does sometimes make me want to die. Or if not die then at least put the book down and pick up something less self-consciously trying to come off as natural, something that isn't so obviously, painfully, "written."

What's wrong with writers these days? Just speak, memory. No one cares about you. If you have something interesting to say, say it. We'll hear it just fine. Use your tongue, it's strong enough. We don't need the rest of you, your parents and cousins and friends and friends' friends. Your tongue is enough, let it waggle in the wind.

Attached to the Pacific

Among much else in Ross Macdonald's (i.e., Kenneth Millar's) long and short fiction featuring detective Lew Archer, fans can pleasurably anticipate the appearance of seen-better-days motels and motor courts the likes of Topanga Court, "a collection of peeling stucco buildings huddled between the Pacific Coast Highway and the eroding cliff" (*Sleeping Beauty*); seen-better-days desk clerks, the likes of which wear badly fitting "brown toupees," their eyes "glazed and solemn with stupidity" (*The Zebra-Striped Hearse*); stopovers at Archer's Los Angeles office on Sunset to browse neglected mail and unpaid bills; famished, forgot-to-eat breakfast feeds of steak and eggs; unconsciousness delineated ("I swung in black space . . . realized with some embarrassment that the body on the deck belonged to me . . . climbed air down to it and crawled back in, a rat who lived in a scarecrow," *The Barbarous Coast*); nightmares revisited ("I was due to arrive someplace . . . but when I went out to my car it had no wheels," *The Underground Man*); unwelcome mirror reminders ("I looked like a ghost from the present haunting a bloody moment in the past," *The Chill*); California truisms ("The wet pavements were almost empty of people, as they always were when it rained in California," *The Far Side of the Dollar*); America truisms ("Like most Americans, I was a counter-puncher," *Instant Enemy*); the aging of dreams and the bodies that were supposed to live them; generational damage and guilt ("The current of guilt flowed in a closed circuit if you traced it far enough," *The Doomsters*); and, most reliably, evocative descriptions of California's oceanic neighbor, which Coleridge scholar Millar preferred to call "the sea."

The sea, as Millar writes it and Archer perceives it, serves as border, soundtrack, eyewitness, trysting locale, body dumpster, mood reflector, a sight-and-sound reminder of the unknown and unknowable, its vastness, moment by moment, putting mere land dwellers in their minuscule universal place. "The cab turned off U.S. 101 in the direction of the sea" begins *The Moving Target*, the first of the Archer novels, and in the seventeen Archer novels that followed, the Pacific maintains its primacy and its "changing blue mystery" (*Black Money*), winking, wrinkling, glaring, roaring under cottages, sucking at pilings, its waters "paved . . . with broken moonlight" (*The Wycherly Woman*), its waves rising like "apparitions" (*The Barbarous Coast*), rolling like "measured installments of eternity" (*The Blue Hammer*) to shores where sunbathers "lie around in the sand like bodies after a catastrophe" (*The Zebra-Striped Hearse*).

Murderers and their victims come and go; the Pacific remains, Lew Archer's constant companion and frequent point of comparison as the detective seeks to unravel tawdry truth. From the story "The Sinister Habit":

"Past his narrow cormorant skull I could see the sky and the sea, wide and candid, flecked with the purity of sails. I spent too much of my time trying to question liars in rented rooms." From the story fragment "Stolen Woman": "I closed my eyes and deliberately rolled over with my face to the wall, telling myself that it was just the sea. I'd been in the beach house for less than a week, and I wasn't used to the constant sound of it."

A California native who came of age in Canada, Kenneth Millar bonded early with the ocean. In 1919, his Canadian father, John Macdonald Millar, moved the family back to Canada and that same year took his four-year-old son on a boat ride that introduced a "shining oceanic world," Millar disclosed in *Self-Portrait*, a collection of criticism and autobiographical sketches. "The Pacific . . . always lapped like blue eternity at the far edge of my life." In 1946, a father himself, Millar reversed his earlier journey, resettling in California with his wife, the crime novelist Margaret Millar, and their young daughter, Linda. It was Margaret who chose the town of Santa Barbara, and it was Margaret's book earnings that paid for the Bath Street house, the first of the Millars' five Santa Barbara residences. Despite the precariousness of the household's income, the Millars at once joined the Coral Casino Beach and Cabana Club on Channel Drive. It was Kenneth Millar's daily habit to swim in both the ocean and the Coral's expansive pool, recreations Richard Moore filmed for his "Writer in America: Ross Macdonald" television documentary. Jill Krementz photographed the trim, wet-haired Millar in plaid bathing trunks, smiling at the camera, dashing along the beach and body surfing on a breaking wave. In Pacific waters, Millar got his "best ideas for books" and often, while swimming "wrote whole paragraphs" (Tom Nolan, *Ross Macdonald: A Biography*). When Eudora Welty, with whom Millar formed a late-life attachment ("an emotional relationship of *great* importance," according to writer Reynolds Price), flew in from Mississippi to keynote the Santa Barbara Writers Conference, Millar met her plane and "in that soft California dark," in Welty's phrase, escorted her on a late-night stroll alongside the Pacific (Nolan).

Millar did not settle on Ross Macdonald, the pseudonym that stuck, until 1956 and the publication of his twelfth book and sixth Lew Archer novel. About the character that brought the other writer in the family fame and fortune, Millar wrote: "Throughout its history . . . the detective hero has represented his creator and carried his values into action in society . . . I wasn't Archer, exactly, but Archer was me" (*Self-Portrait*). Nearer the end of his writing career, he offered a slightly different take on the conjunction, musing that Archer could "possibly" be an "imaginary self-portrait . . . a shadow portrait," the "basic difference" being "I sit in a chair and write, and he gets out and acts." Millar also shared his characterization protocol: "By saying a bit less about a character you can actually tell more" (Paul Nelson and Kevin Avery, *It's All One Case*).

The "bit less" Millar supplied for his Archer character includes a rocky youth as "street boy," "gang-fighter, thief" and "frightened junior-grade hoodlum in Long Beach" (*The Doomsters*). Archer's Contra Costa grandmother had wanted him to become a priest; instead, the reformed street boy became a Long Beach cop and married man. Neither job nor marriage lasted. Ex-wife Sue reasonably expected "a husband she could count on to be there" (*The Goodbye Look*). As a bachelor/detective, Archer presides over a slim bank account, lives in an apartment complex in LA and feeds "his" scrub jays peanuts (*The Underground Man*). Among those whom he actively dislikes: actors, the rich, those who despoil landscapes and people determined to get what they want no matter the collateral cost. Accused in *The Far Side of the Dollar* of having "a secret passion for justice," Archer counters that, no, what drives him is a "secret passion for mercy." As a day-to-day behavioral guide, Millar's detective ascribes to: "Never tell anyone more than he needs to know, because he'll tell somebody else" (*The Blue Hammer*).

In 1964, Santa Barbara's Coyote Fire came within a few hundred yards of the Millars' Chelham Way house. Margaret and the dogs safely evacuated, Millar stayed behind, hosing down the roof, hoping to save their property. The Millars were lucky; a last-minute wind shift sent the fire in another direction and their house, unlike the houses of some of their neighbors, was spared. In *The Underground Man*, Lew Archer also witnesses an out-of-control conflagration. Millar's private eye has been privy to shark-nibbled, bullet-ridden, knife-slashed corpses and a full array of the sordid,

squalid ravages inflicted upon the living, but only once in the series does Archer admit to "shock," a reaction to the sight and threat of engulfing flames. "I glanced up at the mountains, and was shocked by what I saw. The fire had grown and spread as if it fed on darkness" (*The Underground Man*). In that novel, the sixteenth title in the series, biographer Matthew Brucolli discerns an "older and tired" Archer. "Other people's tragedies have wearied him" (*Ross Macdonald*). If, as Wendy Lesser posits in *Pictures at an Execution*, "the murder story must do its best to answer all the answerable questions, and still leave something open or unresolved in the end," the fictional Archer narratives leave unresolved what is never resolved for humankind: sorrow, regret, the inability to undo what has been done.

The heir apparent to Dashiell Hammett and Raymond Chandler, Millar never lost his respect and admiration for Hammett; Chandler was another matter. How much of the pedestal slippage was precipitated by Chandler's harsh criticism of Millar's own work (*The Moving Target*, Chandler famously quipped, could be used "as a springboard for a sermon on How Not to Be a Sophisticated Writer") is open to speculation. Millar demoted Chandler for having a "vision" that lacked "the tragic unity of Hammett's" and considered Chandler's "The Simple Art of Murder" essay a "not very illuminating" guide to the genre (*Self-Portrait*). In general, so-called hard-boiled detective fiction on closer examination contained quite a bit of "lyrical" content, Millar argued. "You might call it romanticism of the proletariat," he explained to a *National*

Observer reporter. Of his own style in particular, he said: "I'm not just interested in a simile for the sake of what it does in the sentence. I'm interested in what it does in terms of the whole book. Some of my similes . . . carry the message of my book better than anything else I write" (*Self-Portrait*).

Nettled whenever reviewers described his work as "Chandleresque," Millar believed his literary range "exceeded" Chandler's. "There's a whole element in my work which . . . doesn't appear . . . in Chandler, and that's the psychological/symbolic aspect of the action and the imagery" (Nelson and Avery). He also believed his series had legs. After turning in his second Archer manuscript, *The Drowning Pool*, he predicted to editor Alfred Knopf: "I have an idea that Archer as he becomes known will do quite well for us." He placed a high value on his wife's work as well. Given the opportunity, Millar extravagantly praised Margaret's novels, reiterating that he considered her simply "the best in the business" (Bruccoli). Margaret did not repay the compliment. When Diana Cooper-Clark came to Santa Barbara to interview both authors for *Designs of Darkness: Interviews with Detective Novelists*, Margaret made plain her contempt for the same-detective format, dissing, by implication, the bulk of her husband's output. Although it might help her sales to feature "the same detective the way Ken has," she'd be "bloody well bored" by the repetition. "I don't think you can write many books about a detective without repeating yourself *ad nauseam*," Margaret told Cooper-Clark. "It's a hell of a lot harder to create a new detective every time."

Marked in its early years by physical violence on both sides, the Millars' marriage proved to be a difficult, volatile union. Margaret did not disguise her disdain for her husband's academic ambitions and his pursuit of a doctorate from the University of Michigan, which she considered a waste of time. While he struggled to find his niche, she felt "trapped" by marriage and more so by motherhood (Nolan). They were a couple at odds in the bedroom: he wanted more sex; she, less. They were also a household, first to last, of unequal incomes, a partnership inevitably complicated by acknowledged or unacknowledged feelings of competition, given the impossibility of two writers simultaneously enjoying peak professional success. And then there was their troubled daughter, Linda.

Born in Kitchener, Ontario, the year after her parents married, Linda Jane Millar grew to be a smart, pretty, precocious, willful child and teenager who felt out of place in Santa Barbara and neglected by her famous parents, despite what others perceived as her father's idealization of and devotion to his daughter. Like many other teenagers, she smoked, drank, had sex and denied she engaged in those pastimes when caught. Curiously, her psychologically astute father insisted that his child never lied and routinely defended her version of events. On a rainy February night in 1956, driving drunk in the Ford Tudor her father had gifted her, sixteen-year-old Linda struck two thirteen-year-old pedestrians on a Santa Barbara street, killing Ernest Dal Zuffo and severely injuring Michael Perona. Driving on, she smashed into a parked Buick, the second collision flipping her own car. Linda's subsequent arrest and trial exposed the Millars' private lives to public scrutiny, ridicule and resentment. The family was accused of receiving preferential treatment from police and courts, Millar and Margaret of being bad parents and alcoholics themselves. Out on bail, Linda slashed her wrists and was soon committed to the State Hospital in Camarillo. After a sentence, with restrictions, of eight years probation, the family fled Santa Barbara for Menlo Park. As did his daughter, Millar saw a therapist in Menlo Park. He described the results of those sessions in terms aquatic: "My half-suppressed Canadian years, my whole childhood and youth, rose like a corpse from the bottom of the sea to confront me" (*Self-Portrait*). Among the painful memories: his father's abandonment of the family, his mother's dire financial situation thereafter, Millar's last-minute reprieve from life in an orphanage when his father's cousin agreed to take him in, an unsettled, rootless existence throughout his teens. It was a past that left many scars and a lasting residue of bitterness. Asked in 1976 what he considered to be his "worst" personal characteristic, Millar named "anger in all its forms." The "structure of any one of my books is a conflict between the rawest forces of life and a very stringent, intellectual control," he told Paul Nelson. "Is that also true of your own life?" Nelson probed. "I

suspect so," Millar answered (*It's All One Case*).

With Linda off to college at UC Davis, Margaret and Millar gave in to their coastal longing and quietly returned to Santa Barbara, renting a house that overlooked the Pacific on Camino de la Luz. It was a short-lived idyll of peace. Once again, for reasons other than novels, the Millar family found themselves in the public eye. On May 30, 1959, Linda failed to return to her dorm by curfew; for more than a week she went missing. A desperate, sleep-deprived Millar personally searched for his daughter, hired detectives, made media appeals for information and direct appeals to his daughter, urging her to come home. Eventually found at a Reno bar, Linda only vaguely remembered what had transpired after parting ways with the two male companions who'd originally accompanied her to Harrah's casino on the Nevada border. Millar told the Santa Barbara *News-Press* that he believed his daughter had suffered "some kind of psychic break." After the ordeal, an exhausted Millar was hospitalized, diagnosed with severe hypertension and heart damage. As soon as he was physically able, he returned to his swimming routine. Linda also regained some measure of equilibrium, married and had a son. But she continued to have struggles with alcohol and needed Seconal to sleep. Following her death at age 31, her parents buried her ashes in Santa Barbara Cemetery, "above the beach where she took her first swim in the Pacific," her grieving father wrote to a family friend. "She was a strong swimmer in her day." Without exception,

Millar refused to answer questions about Linda in interviews; that no such questions be broached became a precondition of his consent. Even so, the family trauma worked its way into Margaret's and Millar's fictions. In the Archer series, *The Galton Case*, *The Chill* and most prominently *Sleeping Beauty* all feature Linda-like characters, lost and unhappy young women who, as Linda had said of herself, "tried" to grow up, but "didn't do well" (Nolan).

Once Millar hit his stride as a novelist, he typically wrote four hours a day in longhand on a pine writing board held in his lap, seated in a red "imitation leather" armchair that Margaret had bought for him in 1946 (Nelson and Avery). A man once able to recite poetry and lengthy passages of prose in perfect detail, Millar began experiencing memory lapses as early as 1971. In revising *Sleeping Beauty*, he confused days of the week in the book's timeline, an error corrected by editors at Knopf. By 1976, the year his eighteenth and final Archer novel, *The Blue Hammer*, was published, he was repeating entire sentences in his correspondence. In interviews he avoided proper names and the titles of his books, referring to *Sleeping Beauty* as "my book about the oil spill." In 1979, to a younger correspondent, Millar turned again to water imagery to explain his plight: "My own personal tides are not as strong and dependable as I would like them to be." Nevertheless, he continued to grant interviews, the last to Diana Cooper-Clark, conducted at the Coral. "Within five minutes it was absolutely clear something awful was happening," Cooper-Clark said. "He was doing the best that he could. And it was horrible . . . because he was such a dignified man. It's like the musician going deaf, the painter going blind."

Millar was diagnosed with Alzheimer's in 1981; Margaret made public his condition in a *Los Angeles Times* article published in 1982. "He knows what's happening to him most of the time, but he doesn't really feel things," she told the reporter. As the person primarily responsible for his care: "I lose my temper and then I go on guilt trips," she admitted. "The trips aren't as big as they used to be, but the temper remains the same." A year before Millar's death, long put off by Margaret and warned that Millar wouldn't recognize her, Eudora Welty arrived in Santa Barbara to see "Ken" and judge the situation herself. Despite being "appalled" by what she viewed as Margaret's insensitive and punitive treatment of Millar and heartbroken by his diminishment, Welty was glad she'd made the effort because "he *did* know me," she told Tom Nolan. As Welty watched Millar, aided by a helper, swim laps in the Coral's pool, she felt grateful that he hadn't been deprived of everything he loved. He "still remembered how to swim," she said. And, as ever, swimming "did him good."

WHEN EVERYTHING'S FEARSOME, NOTHING'S FRIGHTENING.

Kurt Luchs

Vaya Con Vaudeville

Where the Golden Age of Comedy Came from and What It Can Teach Us

What did Hollywood's Golden Age comedians and filmmakers do, exactly? More importantly, why and how were they able to do it? Why has no one been able to do it quite like that since then? And what, if anything, can these funny people teach us about vice and virtue, and the role of psyche and spirit in artistic creation? Is their comedy in any way redemptive, compared to the comedy of today, and does that even matter?

Or are those all loaded questions? Was there really a Golden Age of film comedy? Isn't now a Golden Age? Aren't we surrounded by more comedy and comedians now than ever before in human history? Look at the sheer proliferation of standup shows, improv shows, sketch shows, and that most American of comedic staples, the sitcom. Not to mention today's film industry, which industriously cranks out things it calls comedies every week—things with titles like "Jackass Forever", "Hocus Pocus 2" and "Legally Blonde 3." After all, humor is so subjective. Who's to say these cine-matic confections will not be regarded as classics 50 or 100 years from now? What's more, classics that can teach us just as much about the world we live in, the human condition, and yes, vice and virtue, as the comedies of some mythical Golden Age?

Who's to say? I am.

I've spent a lifetime studying comedy in all of its forms, in all of its historic phases. I've spent decades writing comedy for all mediums. Like many honest, thinking persons who have made this journey through America's ways of being funny, I have concluded that there was indeed a Golden Age of screen comedy. In fact, the conclusion is so glaringly obvious as to be inescapable. If we were on Zoom right now, I could gladly prove it to you with a collection of unrivalled film clips, and this essay would become not merely instructive but highly entertaining.

As it is, for the sake of argument we will have to assume the premise of the Golden Age as a given. I will use this time instead to tell you what and when the Golden Age was, who created it, why their work resonates so much more meaningfully with a healthy spiritual worldview, and why, sadly, we will never see their like again. And lest you feel completely cheated, yes, along the way I will touch on vice and virtue.

I wish I could forego a brief history lesson, but frankly this era is now so completely forgotten that it is necessary to recap it a bit in order for you to make sense of the rest of my essay.

Film as a medium was invented in the late 19th century. It became a popular art form in the first decade of the 20th century, and by the second decade it began to discover its own potential for the intersection of popular art with high art. D.W. Griffith's *Birth of a Nation* is generally regarded as the turning point (never mind the racism, ugh!). Soon film comes to resemble the other great American inventions in popular art which mix high and low with such gusto: the comic strip, jazz, the Broadway musical, and more recently rock and roll.

Depending on how you define it, the Golden Age of screen comedy began in about 1915 and lasted 30 years, until roughly 1945.

It started with Charlie Chaplin around 1915. It continued with Harold Lloyd, Harry Langdon and especially Buster Keaton and Laurel & Hardy in the 1920s. Then came Al Jolson and sound in *The Jazz Singer*. If you've seen *Singing in the Rain*, you've seen a nostalgic comic perspective on the chaos this caused. But there was nothing comic to the artists whose careers vanished overnight. Chaplin was virtually finished. First he made a couple of sound features that were really silent films with music and sound effects (*City Lights* and *Modern Times*). Then he simply self-destructed as an artist, silenced by the death of his natural medium, the silent film. Buster Keaton was also destroyed both professionally and personally, descending into alcoholism and madness, both of which I'm happy to say he eventually recovered from. Langdon

and Lloyd were totally erased from memory. The only silent comedians who made the transition to sound seamlessly, becoming even more successful than before, were Laurel & Hardy.

The Golden Age of screen comedy in the 1930s centered around three distinctly different forms of genius: the now-talking Laurel & Hardy, the maniacal anarchy of the Marx Brothers, and the misanthropic misadventures of W.C. Fields, in my opinion the greatest comic mastermind on film. Then in the mid-1930s a new kind of screen comedy appeared—screwball comedy—which depended more on the writer and director and where the major roles were usually taken by actors, not comedians. Some say the first screwball comedy was *Twentieth Century* directed by Howard Hawks in 1934. Some say it was *My Man Godfrey* directed by Gregory LaCava in 1936. Interestingly, they both starred Carole Lombard, so one thing everyone can agree on is that she was the first screwball actress.

By 1940 every one of the original Golden Age comedians had either stopped producing good work or stopped working altogether. Screwball comedies were now the main venue for humor in Hollywood. Howard Hawks and Gregory LaCava were joined by such brilliant directors as George Cukor, who gave us *Holiday* and *The Philadelphia Story*, Frank Capra, who did *You Can't Take It with You* and *Arsenic and Old Lace*, and Ernest Lubitsch, who did Carole Lombard's final film, *To Be or Not to Be* (NOT the Mel

Brooks version!). But the one creator of screwball comedies whose name outshines all others is Preston Sturges, the first filmmaker in Hollywood (after Chaplin) to receive a writer-director credit. Sturges made *Sullivan's Travels*, *The Lady Eve*, and half a dozen other incomparable comedies in just five short years, then for all intents and purposes simply vanished from the face of the earth. Although I consider Sturges the finest comedic screenwriter of all time, I'm afraid that the screwball comedy portion of the Golden Age will get short shrift here. Again, there just isn't time, and for reasons that will become apparent, it falls outside the main focus of my essay.

The end of the Golden Age was nearly as glorious as the beginning. It was the "Road" pictures starring Bob Hope, Bing Crosby and Dorothy Lamour, starting with *The Road To Singapore* in 1940 and continuing on with *The Road To Zanzibar*, *The Road To Morocco*, and on and on into the 1950s and even a comeback picture in 1962, *The Road To Hong Kong*, which should be avoided at all costs. The "Road" pictures that matter were made in the 1940s. Hope also starred in a number of great solo comedies, and if all you know of him is his watered-down television specials or his USO shows, you don't know Bob Hope at all. At his best, he was one of the best.

How strange—and yet, given all this, how understandable—that the same Golden Age comedians who conquered vaudeville and then film were also the pioneers of radio and television comedy. I'm thinking of Jack Benny, Milton Berle, and Burns and Allen, among so many others. Fields did vaudeville, film and radio (the latter most memorably with Edgar Bergen and Charlie McCarthy), and he would've done television too if he didn't drink himself to death in 1946. In a way, he did do television anyway in 1933, because the then-new invention was the focus of the film *International House*, which he steals from all of his co-stars.

So much for the historical outline.

The comedy of the Golden Age is a better embodiment of a healthy spiritual worldview largely because, like Christianity as originally conceived, it is incarnational: that is, it embraces the physical without demeaning or degrading the spiritual. By contrast, the comedy of today either ignores or downplays the physical, or embraces the physical while demeaning both it and the spiritual.

One example: Charlie Chaplin's Little Tramp yearns for love and sex, in that order, though the sex is merely implied and we never see him get any. The characters on *Two and a Half Men*—or almost any other contemporary sitcom or film—yearn for sex, sex, sex, and sex, in that order. They do more than yearn for sex, they get it endlessly, in endless combinations, with anyone who happens to be handy, without reference to the characters or to the character of the characters. But despite their apparent embrace of the physical, the focus is on their talk. And the tone of their talk is demeaning—leering and suggestive without being truly witty or insightful. Instead of a carefully crafted human comedy that is about the whole person, and which can engage our whole person, we get a loosely connected stream of wisecracks aimed at one organ—unfortunately, not the heart or the brain. One wants to say to the writers, in the words of Gandalf to the Balrog, "You shall not pass!"

Incidentally, I must add for those who might infer that I am some sort of prude, no, I am not. I enjoy the profane in humor as much as anyone. I love Lenny Bruce, both the early clean Lenny and the later dirty Lenny. I enjoy the *Hangover* movies, vulgarity and all, mostly because they have a lot of heart as well as a lot of smut. And I yield to no one in my adoration of Derek and Clive (Peter Cook and Dudley Moore), because the profanity and filth emerge largely from the mind of the most intelligent and talented comedian ever born, Cook, and along with the filth there is always genuine wit and insight. Louis C.K. he most definitely is not. Of course in an age of wokeness run amok Pete and Dud are totally beyond the pale, even in their cleaner material, and I will perhaps be hung up by my thumbs for mentioning them.

Even when it is artfully done, the physical humor of the Golden Age frequently encounters an irrational prejudice from contemporary viewers. It has often been said that the two lowest forms of humor are puns and slapstick. Whoever said that didn't know anything about humor. A brilliant pun is brilliant. The fact that it's a pun is irrelevant. By the same token, not only is slapstick not a lower order of humor, but properly done it is perhaps the most difficult form of humor to pull off. If you think it's easy to lie sideways on the floor while doing windmills with your feet and going "Woo woo woo woo woo!" like Curly of the Three Stooges, think again. Or check out Buster Keaton in his masterpiece *The General*, a silent Civil War comedy that takes place mostly on a hijacked runaway train. There are a few camera tricks, but for the most part Keaton is doing his own stunts, live—amazing, hilarious, unbelievable stunts that no stuntman would dare do today, let alone a leading man. The unions and insurers would never allow it.

Yet slapstick is frequently looked down upon for being so, well, physical. I sense an elitist, Gnostic impulse in such sneering. And in both cases it is an impulse to reject the truth of life on earth. The slapstick of the Golden Age comedians reminds us again and again that we are creatures with bodies. Because we are fallen creatures in a fallen world, much of their humor comes from what happens to our bodies when our fallenness catches up with us. To be fully incarnational in such a world is to be taught over and over that pride and vanity and stupidity goeth before a fall—literally.

Another bugaboo about slapstick that arises from our contemporary plague of political correctness is that it is too violent. No kidding! Yet what the thought police seem to miss is that slapstick violence—at least the Golden Age kind—is cathartic without being deadly. Just as in a Roadrunner cartoon, characters are almost never killed or even seriously injured by slapstick, even when anvils fall on them or when Oliver Hardy runs the teeth of a saw across Stan Laurel's head. Indeed, in so many of these Golden Age comedies we can feel the sheer joyfulness, the exuberance that accompanies the often-outrageous physical clowning. It is the uniquely worldly spiritual joy of reveling in the body . . . even a body that sometimes walks through plate glass windows for our amusement.

Not to stretch the parallels too far, but in their denial of the finality of death, these comedies contain more than a hint of resurrection as well. There is a reason why Dante called his magnum opus "The Divine Comedy."

Something needs to be said about another aspect of the slapstick that resonates with the spiritual virtues: its fundamental dignity. I know that seems paradoxical, and I don't mean it to be, but I'm talking about the way classic slapstick is performed. When two or more Golden Age characters are inflicting outrageous actions upon each other—cutting off each other's ties, spraying each other with garden hoses, slapping each other with loaded paint brushes—the humor is greatly heightened by the deliberate, measured way in which these insults are usually delivered.

One example: In the Laurel & Hardy two-reeler *Towed In A Hole*, when Ollie

wants to pour cold water inside Stan's overalls, he fills the bucket, gives Stan the bucket to hold . . . and Stan holds it! Meanwhile, Ollie gets a piece of wood so he can prop the front of Stan's overalls open while he pours the water in. In classic slapstick style, Stan watches these proceedings with interest, but no alarm. When the tables are turned and Stan is inflicting an outrage on Ollie, the result is the same. It is still a tooth for a tooth and an eye for an eye, but a very dignified, unflappable eye for an eye.

Of course all this makes the comedy funnier, but it has another effect, too. It is almost a way of saying, This is how to meet the outrages of life: with dignity, with civility even in our fallenness and our desire for revenge, and with a smile.

The incarnational aspect of Golden Age comedy leads us ineluctably to other questions that must be asked, such as: why is this comedy so artfully physical? How did it get that way? Why is there almost nothing like it today? And here we get to the heart of our subject.

The answer is simple yet to our age mysterious: vaudeville. Before DVDs or Blu-rays, before streaming, before television, before radio, before film, there was vaudeville. For decades, vaudeville was the main means by which people across the country could see something more entertaining than their own family members (in England it was the music hall, a similar yet different tradition). It was an immense traveling theatrical circuit, with stages in almost every American town, and several key impresarios and many smaller ones in charge of booking the talent.

And what did that talent consist of? Imagine one of the old television variety hours like the *Ed Sullivan Show* or the *Dean Martin Show*, only two or three times as long, with no commercials, and anywhere from a dozen to several dozen very diverse acts on the bill: singers and musical groups of every age, gender and nationality; dancers; magicians; jugglers; acrobats; novelty acts; animal acts; serious actors doing everything from brief monologues to entire plays; and yes, comedians.

It's no accident that every one of the original Golden Age comedians got their start in vaudeville. Their screen personas were all formed in vaudeville. All of them brought their most successful vaudeville sketches and bits of business to the screen, sometimes repeatedly. The famous golf sketch of W.C. Fields is performed in no less than four different films! Such was his love for the vaudeville stage that Fields even incorporated large parts of the vaudeville staple "The Drunkard"—originally a 19th century morality play—into his film *The Old Fashioned Way*, which is itself a fascinating look at the vaudevillian's life on the road.

The Old Fashioned Way is one of the precious few direct documents we have of what vaudeville was like. Another is the biographical picture *The Great Ziegfeld*, which includes both authentic and recreated vaudeville performances. The connection is that

each year impresario Florenz Ziegfeld cherry-picked the best of vaudeville and brought it to Broadway in his perennial Ziegfeld's Follies.

In a very real sense, however, all the comedies of the Golden Age are simply the antics of vaudeville transferred to the new medium and captured forever on celluloid. The first Golden Age comedian, Charlie Chaplin, was born in Britain but got his start in American vaudeville. Guess who his vaudeville understudy was? Another Englishman, Stan Laurel. As a child, Buster Keaton was part of a family vaudeville troupe whose act concluded by throwing young Buster into the orchestra pit. What physical stunt for a film could possible scare him after that?

But so what? Who cares where these comedians learned their art? What difference could this accident of history possibly make to the quality of their work? It makes all the difference. There are three primary reasons why.

The first key thing about vaudeville, as opposed to starting out as a comedian in today's standup or improv comedy clubs, is that you had to entertain an entire theater full of people, most of whom probably had not come to see you, or even to see comedy in general. This is a completely different level of challenge from a comedian in a comedy club today, where people come expecting or at least hoping to laugh. To meet the challenge of vaudeville, a comedian had to make his or her work as universal as possible, and that meant using every weapon in his arsenal, including every funny thing he could do with his body.

The vaudeville performers had a built-in advantage in meeting the challenge. Fortunately, the solution was partly contained within the problem. If you think of vaudeville as a kind of showbiz university, everyone on this very diverse bill was in effect getting a free master class in every conceivable type of performing art. This is one of the main reasons the vaudevillians are so well rounded when they get to the silver screen. The singers learned how to juggle and tell jokes. The comedians learned how to dance and sing and mime. Conversely, in today's comedy clubs, the six or seven comedians on the bill get to see six or seven other comedians who are very much like themselves. They learn nothing. We don't learn much from those who are exactly like us. Diversity is built into the very structure of reality. It's foundational. The only entertainment outlet offering anything like this kind of diverse education today is Cirque du Soleil.

A second key aspect of vaudeville was that it took many years to rise to the top, far longer than it does in today's fast-moving multimedia entertainment world. Both the Marx Brothers and W.C. Fields spent decades in vaudeville honing their craft. Fields didn't utter a word in his first 15 years on-stage! He was a silent comic juggler, the most famous one in the world. He and the other vaudevillians spent decades in front of every kind of audience, in every size of city, in every area of the country, at every hour of the day or night. Decades following every kind of act, including some of the biggest stars of their day. (Incidentally, the one act W.C. Fields admitted he could not follow was the Marx Brothers. As he put it, when they finished with an audience, there were no laughs left in them.) The long climb to the top meant that vaudeville performers didn't generally achieve fame until they were hitting on all cylinders and doing their best work. This is a far cry from someone like Jim Carrey becoming famous for something like *Ace Ventura*.

The virtue in question here, of course, is patience. No matter how long it may last, life on earth is a marathon for anyone interested in following a spiritual path, the path every genuine artist is on for sure. Sprinting will not get it done. There is much we can learn in this regard from the plucky vaudeville troopers who became the great Golden Age comedians.

Finally, unlike film or radio or television, vaudeville did not constantly chew up material. In vaudeville you didn't keep changing your act every week or even every year. Most performers toured with the exact same act for years, or again, even decades. Rather than making performers stagnant or uninventive, this had the counterintuitive effect of making them absolute masters of their craft. It was like Glenn Gould practicing Bach's *Goldberg Variations* for his entire life. When he died, you can be sure he knew that piece of music better than anyone on earth. And because of that, mysteriously, he knew music itself better than anyone on earth. The same could be said of Monet and his water lilies, or Oliver Hardy and his pratfalls.

This discipline, this doggedness and determination that marked the great vaudevillians who became the great Golden Age comedians, has tremendous implications for the spiritual life, particularly in the avoidance of vice and the pursuit of virtue. We do not wake and greet the world each morning eager to practice some novel and yet-to-be-revealed collection of virtues. Each day, if we are decent human beings made of anything more solid than tissue paper, we seek to know truth and to love our neighbors as ourselves. Two simple, easily comprehended tasks. And yet they are the hardest things any human being will ever do, and if we perform this bit of material every day for the rest of our lives, we will die still not having learned everything there is to know about it.

The fact that the vaudevillians didn't change their act every week has another impact on the film comedy they ended up created during the Golden Age. While these films are very much of their time, and frequently contain a number of topical and politically incorrect references, they are not topical in the sense that almost all comedy is today. That's another whole essay, a very sad one, and you won't read it today. The point is, the Golden Age comedies tend to be based on universal human needs and concerns and

situations, and their humor revolves around universal truths of human nature. And this makes their humor not only universal, but evergreen. Chaucer would have loved it.

And in fact, the Golden Age comedians have much more in common with Chaucer and Shakespeare and Dickens and Austen than they do with the comedy of today. For one thing, unlike our 21st century comedians, who seem to have studied only the collected works of Hugh Hefner and Larry Flynt, the Golden Age comedians had actually read the great writers. Neither W.C. Fields nor Groucho Marx finished high school, let alone college, but both of them traveled with trunks full of books and spent most of their free time reading. Fields was a friend and frequent guest of H.L. Mencken, arguably the most learned man of letters of his generation, and a man whose inimitable prose style exerted a major influence on every intelligent person who had anything to do with comedy.

A word should be said about the technical medium of the Golden Age comedies, black-and-white celluloid. There are many people today who find it difficult to watch black-and-white films, because black-and-white means "old," and "old" is bad, or because the world is in color, and black-and-white isn't a fitting way to depict reality. Yet I find in black-and-white another Golden Age paradox and another parallel to the healthy spiritual life. Just as silent comedies are universal because they transcend the barriers of language, black-and-white comedies are universal because they eliminate nonessentials and allow us to focus on what matters. What matters in a comedy is character, situation, timing, laughs, the element of surprise—not costumes, color, set design or cinematography. I contend that the people in a black-and-white film are one step closer to being universal archetypes just by virtue of the medium itself.

In a similar way, part of the genius of the great spiritual leaders is not simply that they tell the truth, but that they tell the most essential truth, the black-and-white truth that we so often seem to miss: the reality of our finite, fallen and often misdirected nature, and the necessity of turning away from that and walking into the light (whatever that is for you) to achieve anything worthwhile in life. Everything else is window dressing. It's a nice sort of validation that nearly all major religions and philosophies share a similar moral code, the same golden rule.

Some might consider the art of film comedy to be a lowly one. I do not. Like Shakespeare—with whom, obviously, I have very little else in common—I feel comedy occupies a role as central as tragedy and history (if indeed those are separate things). Whenever we want to be reminded of the joys of it at its very best, the work of the Golden Age comedians is there. They have joined the immortals and are busy giving a hot foot to the gods.

Tomoé Hill

First, a Feeling

On Translation Without Language

I have no aptitude for languages. To be kind, I might, but not in the standard manner. My vocabulary is luxuriant but mostly with nouns as they pertain to perfume, food, or drink: Framboise, pino, ménta, rōzu. Breaking my way through sentences as if they were winter's frozen-over waters, shards clinging to my lips, I remain a monoglot. It is not for lack of trying. Throughout my life there were sometimes years-long attempts at acquiring everything from Japanese to Latin. My brain cannot make the complex connections that result in mastered languages, an issue I also experience with structured learning. What I have is like pebbles gathered on a beach, fragments of a tongue. I have partially hidden this, reading and writing as I do: over the years I have encountered disdain by others who read and write with voracity. Someone without this aptitude is considered less intellectual, unable to truly understand knowledge or beauty. If I am this, so be it. There is still beauty enough for me.

Foreign-language movies have helped. There is something more natural in following a vocal rhythm than subtitles—though they too are useful. It explains why I cannot speak Japanese, but understand my mother perfectly. Like a muscle, memory remembers the rhythm of language as much as its words. What does the co-cooned unborn child understand and communicate to but the rhythms of those who speak the yet-unknown? It is neither speech nor noise in the way we know it, but it nevertheless wakes the gestation-memory, its first intuition. Recently I found myself watching Alain Corneau's *Série noire*, which had no English subtitles. But it was based on Jim Thompson's noir novel *A Hell of a Woman*, and I found the rhythm of the dialogue, though reflecting particular French mannerisms, maintained the unmistakable rhythm of the genre. While necessary to sometimes look up certain words or phrases, the overall story with its nuances of pitch-black humour and pathos was clear.

Afterwards, I knew to someone fluent, they might have argued there was no way I could truly grasp the movie, with my gaps and guessing. I would not disagree; in a way, I fully agree—*I cannot understand the way they do*. But as I do not believe in understanding as necessarily homogenous in language or elsewhere, this hardly seemed an issue. Yes, sometimes I translated correctly, at others what could only be called the gist, my brain somehow connecting over or through the undecipherable. With books, each subsequent translation of a classic is slightly different: each translator's choices and perspective in reading the original change while retaining what we could call, alongside the specifics of plot and character, the general feeling, or again, rhythm. It is feeling that most interests me in language or whatever it is I cannot grasp in learning, but nevertheless find fragments of in my attempts.

The understanding in hindsight that there is some issue, without knowing precisely what that might be, renders the process of learning an island. Addressing learning difficulties or disabilities was much less common when I was a child. Children deemed to have them were literally removed from 'normal' class to a small room for more individual tuition: a place I briefly found myself later, though there was nothing more special about the teaching bar an exceptionally patient teacher minding children of various unspecified needs (behavioural needs were yet another room). I would expect there to be some pushback against the idea that I did or do have issues; after all, I was placed ahead not just once or twice, but three times in my younger schooling life due to a much more advanced reading comprehension. Looking back again, there was much emphasis placed on my ability to process and comprehend as a whole based on that alone, and to address an ever-present elephant, I was a part-Asian child. The assumption was having skill x at a young age meant I would have skills y and z as well. It seemed unthinkable in the early-mid 1980s that an Asian child would have academic difficulties, something that only served to further compound my issues. In a 2016 article titled 'The Road to Higher Education With an "Invisible Disability"' in *The Atlantic*, Laura Castañeda writes: 'Despite what many may believe, learning differences do not correlate to lower intelligence or an intellectual disability.' This is wonderful to know now, but my dilemma remained. How does one navigate learning of any kind knowing they face a structural void—a silence—which others do not?

In Jacques Derrida's essay 'What is a "Relevant" Translation' (tr. Lawrence Venuti), he says, 'What is most often called "relevant"? Well, whatever feels right . . . coming at the moment when you expect it'. This seems vague, but he says earlier, 'there is no such thing as a word in nature'. Now this vagueness assumes a mantle of naturalism. The *word* may not be natural, but to feel—one may even extend this to be an instinct of the communicative animal—is necessary. The requirement of the intangible in translation suddenly renders fractured understanding important. Later, he cites Cicero as someone early in championing this method, saying 'the operation that consists of converting, turning . . . doesn't have to take a text at its word or to take the word literally. It suffices to transmit the idea, the figure, the force.' There is an inherent guesswork in this method. Call it risk or intuition. They are both true, and point to the necessity of the individuality of thought. Translation and learning lives—thrives—on its possibilities.

Derrida's words immediately validated something in how I read certain texts: not even from the viewpoint of translated language, but more intellectual writing and learning generally. As someone who only studied basic classical philosophers and a handful of contemporary ones at university, I had no idea of the vast number of theorists and thinkers: Barthes, Cixous, Benjamin, Stewart, to name a few. It was not until years later and rather organically in my literary wanderings that I encountered them. Not knowing anything of theory or more importantly, the social groupings around them which would become clear via social media, I came to them naively. I was fascinated, awed, charmed, and even angry at times by the writing I was discovering. Naïveté and feeling, as it turned out, became the base upon which to create a structure of my own.

Upon joining social media, it was clear that I did not understand these texts in the way long-time scholars (with or without accreditation) of such works declared one should. I attributed this first to a lack of more advanced education, or a lack of knowing the right kind of people, whatever 'right' meant. The same feelings of learning inadequacy that haunted me through my school and university years reappeared. It became a growing source of worry. Maybe I really could not understand a thing I was reading; after all, it seemed so different to what I was being told I should understand. This is the peculiar and poisonous thinking of cliques, intellectual or otherwise. Perhaps contradictorily, from a sense of intimidation—I did not want to admit I came to these thinkers so late—I continued to read, ignored the should and should nots that dictate so much in a digital age. Sometimes the fear of what you are not becomes the driver of what you become. Still, it occurs to me that the act of referencing Derrida in such a piece as this is both audacious and laughable: the former because I dare to use something that unlike the more studied, I can only understand in fragments, the latter because I simply dare to dare: punching above my intellectual weight in the stubborn belief there is something there for me, too.

I found in these admittedly lonely readings something I called 'emotional translation'. Left out of whatever I could not grasp in discussions of the text, I was left only to trust feeling (and the space to fail without judgement). Where the complexity of terms as a whole eluded me despite knowing individual meanings, I learned to comprehend and contextualise with intuition. Almost always finding something instinctually reminding me of an experience or prior knowledge, I used it tentatively as a cipher's key, which would result in a kind of reverse-engineered understanding. Because of that feeling and trust between myself and the text, not only did I come to be able to 'translate' and learn from them, but in the process discover perspectives I would not have realised had I gone no further than accepting the standard readings as the only ones.

In John le Carré's *Tinker, Tailor, Soldier, Spy*, during the debriefing of the spy Ricki Tarr, he says to George Smiley in regard to the translating of a diary: 'He looked up from his labours and his grin widened. "'To possess another language is to possess another soul.'"' The joke in the book is that Tarr does not know Russian. The diary, never translated, only copied, was written in English by Irina, a Russian spy. If I have no languages, am I left with fragments of souls? What flight is left to those with only stray feathers? The si-lence-language is one of dreams, or perhaps nightmares, for it allows nothing except feeling. But to know other languages is the closest I imagine we get to the true feeling of flight, without materiality. More so, as it moves the whole being in a way the mere physical act of motion could never do. I feel glimpses of this soaring in these fragments, but I have felt it completely in another language altogether, one with no voice at all.

The word is air: everywhere but seemingly nowhere. But it was never the beginning.

Alain Tanner's movie *Dans la ville blanche*, aside from being another without English subtitles, features very little dialogue. What is scattered throughout is divided between French, German, Portuguese, a mere few of English, and I would add to that list, silence. Silence takes the form of the in-between for most of us. Our encounters with it are pauses between words on a page or preceding and following speech. Silence is also finality: those who cannot or choose not to speak. But given space to do so, it becomes its own language, one that requires translating and understanding in the same way other languages or knowledge does. In *Silence* by John Biguenet, he asks, 'is a white page, rather than a dark leaf, better for silence? Or will we allow both unsullied whiteness and unrelieved darkness to serve as contradictory images of silence?'

In Tanner's movie, white and dark linguistic silences dazzle and depress.

Its characters exchange the majority of their dialogue sparely, even without, but still vocal within intimacies that no speech could better articulate. The few words they offer act as punctuation to this secret language: confirmations of freedom and emptiness, pleasure and loss. There is the chaos of everyday noise, but set at an existential distance from Paul, its protagonist. Moving from the dark of a ship's engine room to the unreal light of Lisbon, the logic of sound and language are as backwards as the clock he notices in a bar which counts time the wrong way. In a strange city, he gets by with language fragments, communicating his longings and ecstasies mainly through silence. It becomes the structure upon which he creates a new life. The shards upon Paul's lips, as he attempts to translate himself to others and others to himself, are my own.

The letters and home movies he sends to Élisa, his girlfriend back home, are not unlike Derrida's postcards to the unknown receiver. But with every letter and set of images, she is erased from part of his memory. Paul's scrawled and silent translations of the city where he believes lies his newfound freedom, are replaced by new memories, that of Rosa, his lover. With Rosa there is no writing, no trapped images. They translate as they live, in fragments of silence and pleasure and sometimes spoken language, looking out onto the great expanse of blank water and sunlight. The word is artificial and unnatural, so feeling replaces it in its all-consuming desire for understanding, rewriting and retranslating the same sentences on skin. What is worth deciphering, sending, or receiving but each other in this blank city? Derrida: '*Geschick* is destiny, of course, and therefore everything that touches on the destination as well as on destiny . . . *schicken* is to send, *envoyer* to "expedite," to cause to leave or arrive . . . ' Translations and their lack become a form of destiny, individual divinations marking the arrival or departure of words and people, knowledge and meaning.

In the end, we are left with silence and rhythm, nothings that are not quite an absence, nor yet a full presence—anti-noise and anti-language which are as vocal as their twins, speech and melody. If this sounds clichéd to those with full and unfettered understanding of languages, it is no less an important truth for those of us without—it is what allows us hope in gleaning our knowledge where we may. It is the language of postcards and letters whose words were never uttered, the word as flesh, moving images paradoxically still, broken translations, insurmountable structures, gaps and erasures, the communication of the womb. They all wait for a beginning, as I do, for the feeling of possibility and the possibility of feeling, that will make them whole in their own ways.

Marivn Cohen

The Bowels of Memory

HOW MEMORY GOES OUT WITH THE BOWELS (DIALOGUE)

Is it ever possible to remember things BEFORE you experience the events you AFTERWARDS recall?

No. That's an impossibly wrong sequence. You have to earn the right to remember something, by FIRST experiencing it.

Taking it into your own head?

That gives it a head start in the process of recollection.

But what about the process of elimination?

That's a totally different matter, including direction.

How?

The ass builds up dietary or nutritional bowels, which get rejected backward into the depository called the toilet bowl, which eliminates biological stress by ridding the body of built-up waste matter, preceeded by recognizable urges.

What does that have to do with memory?

I sometimes ask myself that question myself. Anyway, the ass starts the movement for elimination's dumping grounds, which operate entirely apart from memory itself. It's called "separation of functions."

So memory goes forward and elimination goes backwards?

Yes, but the person gets caught in the middle.

The separate processes disentangle themselves categorically?

Mutually getting themselves in each other's way stultifies bodily efficiency. Politically it would be insupportably diasterous.

Oh, politics! There you go again.

CORRECT YOUR BOWELS, SO YOU WON'T EMIT HOWLS INSTEAD OF THE ACTUAL BOWELS

The bowel system is so immaculate
that it's virtually intact-ulate.
It eliminates what's obviously a waste,
to your anal's taste.
Unless you're constipated,
it might be slightly belated.
But then it discharges
the necessary, in full barrages,
starting of course with the largest.
Avoid, however, diarrheia,
which is rightfully to be feared,
in case it gets ugly and smeared.
But if you get constipation,
it deserves your full contemplation,
though it's not a case for the United Nations
battling a case of political inflation.
Maybe the doctor will know what to do
in order to make you say "phew!"
But it's not absurd
if you don't emit a turd.
I know, so respect my word.
It's not a car getting the rejects of a bird
that's too silent to be overheard,
so it won't get a tongue-lash
for flying away in a flash.
Oh where to put waste material
so it won't interfere with your cereal?
Down the toilet bowl
to save everyone's soul
who regard themselves as a functioning
    whole.

ME? OH, I'M ALL RIGHT

People are putting on pretenses,
but they're only a bluffer.
They make as if they're well off,
but actually they suffer.
Other people deprive them of pride
by only seeing their underside.
How can they hold out in society

when their lives are miserable without variety?
They don't even have enough money to
     travel,
so their life is in the process of unravel.
They're despondent, in a suicidal mood.
But why so unceremoniously brood?
Let's just pretend that all is well,
and fool other people to fall under your spell
that nothing is wrong, you're quite all right.
So justify yourself by the way you write.
Don't fall down. Get up and fight.
But you're a powderpuff,
and don't have the right stuff.
Then just pretend and bluff
that things aren't so rough.

THE VARIED LIFE OF JACOB SMULLYAN
CAN BE EITHER CALM OR EBULLIENT

Jacob Smullyan
loves literature and music,
which he finds both amusing
and deeply profound.
This he has frequently found.
He loves the piano's tinkling sound,
and the compiling of many a word,
even if they tend to the absurd.
He enjoys life, marriage, and children,
and his friend Tyler,
who's so worth whiler.
Together they have many a drink
till their spirits either rise or sink.
Which one is the more, I can't think.
My judgement is currently on the blink.

MY POETRY WAS A DISGRACE THAT THE CRITICS DIDN'T EVEN BOTHER TO FACE.
THOSE WHO DID MADE A WRY FACE

I tried to be famous, but failed.
Therefore my ego ailed.

I was graded low on the literary scale.
I sacrificed meaning to rhyme,
two nickels worth to a dime.
Therefore I was forgotten in time
by any serious scholar.
My wounded pride would holler
that the critics had me under-rated.
To inglorious doom was my career fated.
Later it was slightly revived, but belated.
Therefore I'm not considered a poet
by any mediocre standard, but below it.

SELF-CRITICISM / DEFIES WITTICISM.
THE WRITER'S CONFESSION / IS NOW IN THE READER'S POSSESSION

It's so exciting
to do all this writing.
My weakness is too many rhymes
that stumble out of context,
so my concepts don't connect.
It's fun to make myself smile
by the process of humor.
I hope to get praised
by tapping on fame's door.
But I'm not allowed within,
because too much rhyming is a sin,
and my violations add up
when my stories grow corrupt.
I wouldn't put a bet on me
to ramble up fame's tricky tree.
I have too many a flaw
which critics and public can't ignore.
I really forgot what writing is for.
Is it to communicate?
Then I'm shoved out of the gate
and submit to my lonely fate.

James Sallis

The Plan for Your Life

Remember

that you must leap
from whatever window is available
in every building you enter

Remember

that the wind will be strong and
not caring who you are
will take you where it will

Remember

that how you fall has nothing
to do with how you lived
or what you believe

Remember

that the stricken face
you see in windows you fall by
will no longer be yours

Yet More Thoughts

I have some trouble with writing. I want to write more, write a wider cultural history of things I know about (disability/illness, eugenics, dead intellectuals), but everything I write is navel-gazing. I don't like impersonal writing, I'm not adept at it and nor do I want to be. I much prefer memoir and diary as a more direct engagement with ideas, though I can't help but feel anything I write about the pandemic or whatever else is yet more morose navel-gazing, more of me complaining about insoluble problems while pontificating on the fact that I'm very sad and ill. It can tire a reader, and why should they care?

There's a place for this indulgence and I will defend it when it's unfairly chastised by snobs, but there's surely more I can do than repeat the same talk about my own feelings and failings. Or at least I'd want to do this in a way that doesn't feel like I'm retreading the same territory over and over again.

I wrote my memoir (*Neither Weak Nor Obtuse*) in an insular way so it could hint at what my broader ideas are without having to expand so much, given I'm lazy. I don't need to write loads about Czeław Miłosz, for example. I can just say he's an influence.

I might want to write something in an interview format, or a dialogue between me and friends, or travel writing—but travel is still difficult given the facts of my health and the pandemic. I'd hop over to Paris again, visit Raymond Aron's grave (again), stop by a few famous cafés and places I've researched. But I'm too anxious to do that any time soon, and it presents a material risk. I could otherwise write about my experience with The Barbellion Prize and accessing literary and publishing culture, but I'd prefer prompting from others to having to drag it up myself.

Unfortunately, most of my writing happens *in extremis*, which is to say, I'm only really motivated to write anything when I'm very ill, in hospital, etc., and I don't recommend this for the sake of art or anything else. I'd much prefer to have zero creativity and a less acrimonious life than go through a lot of pain and nonsense just to write a book or create something: I abjure the 'suffering artist'.

I'm far too judgmental about my writing. I upset myself when I look back at any previous writing and think how I could have simplified it or made it less verbose or made it less abstract and more straightforward. I don't want to write too plainly or boringly, and I try to make my writing organic and easy, but it still has a pompous quality, or it's littered with mistakes. It's odd that people will excuse prolixity from some authors and have their own nebulous, fashionable tastes about style, and it's hard to navigate this if you're insecure. I get some good reviews of my work, but it doesn't help much. I'm sure concerns like this are common but I'm too solipsistic and indulgent to gauge the mood of other writers. And it matters less what they think. I myself need to feel okay with my life and work—not for the sake of any explicit progress or advancement, but just so I can have some small sense of comfort instead of self-hatred.

I ask, why don't I like myself? It's not for any lack of positive affirmation, or others' exacting standards, or ever being told I'm not good enough. The opposite of that happens. I am always reassured of my own goodness, and I have care and support. I don't feel bad because I'm not succeeding greatly at grand things because I don't want grand things, like a career or status. I want a modest and quiet life and the avoidance of more pain and hassle. My ultimate dream is a quiet Hobbiton *cottagecore* life. I've always held my own work and behaviour to a higher standard and I rarely meet it. I saw somewhere recently that self-hatred was a form of narcissism, which I found perverse. As if I can't be satisfied by my efforts because I should be so much better, as if I could be that? The idea only makes me feel *more* useless. I'm now a narcissist because I'm dissatisfied with my life? I should be satisfied? Fuck off.

I know otherwise that peace is pretty difficult in life, in politics, or anywhere. I don't even want to create something amazing, just something I can be okay with—attesting my existence to me, so I'm not so alone.

Most of what I write becomes repetitive, and I repeatedly face the question of why anyone should write at all when most of what could be said has already

been said, and better than I could express. I think it'd be justifiable if I quit altogether. I don't have much of a good argument for others if they ask me why they should write besides, again, solipsism and emotional ventilation. I find myself and my writing embarrassing and no amount of talk or trying not to care changes this. I need regular praise, like a dog, or I feel sad and useless. How selfish of me.

There's too much information in the world. Worry about the overabundance of new information and data is decades old by now; it only gets more cumbersome each day. The copiousness of information, so much of it extraneous and distracting, is trouble enough—in addition there is the social pressure to consume media and know so much about new events, where it can feel impossible to retreat and relax if one wants to remain at all conscious of truly important developments and have any say. If one doesn't care to have a say, then fine. Plenty say a lot with no care at all for being credible or responsible, and that has always been the case. This is bad enough, and then for even more worry and weariness we have the shaming and extortion of others for failing to keep up to date with absolutely everything, every new development in *the discourse*, every new trend, compounded and aggravated by the development of the technological society (oooh look, he referenced Ellul, isn't he clever . . .)—with its increased pace and new demands. It's possible, if spurious, to think it used to be easier, perhaps less unforgiving, to not know of things, when there was still this extant pressure to be an engaged participant but not so exaggerated by the technological innovation of culture. Not that a reactionary antithesis to this would be much help, or even possible. Worse, people talk as if they really did know everything, with a tone and confidence suggesting so, when with so much more information existing now it's surely the case that proportionally they know even less of all there is to know. It's okay to not know things, to not be privy to everything, and one shouldn't face so much ire for not consuming such a huge quantity of media and information, especially when it's trivial or optional.

Abundance becomes a problem, argumentation online is difficult unless it is heavily curated or moderated; 'debate culture' is overrated, a rhetorical exercise, not a proper *pedagogy*—or in less fancy words, it's not the way one learns and reflects best on ideas. There are too many voices shouting over each other, many with insincere or glib motivations—many more that are plainly uninformed, many others violent—for most to glean any real knowledge or wisdom, and it becomes more difficult to find what is genuinely insightful when it's subsumed by so much vitriol and noise. Unless you're wanting to know the nature of noise! It is better to limit oneself and engage in a broad overview of ideas at some distance, preferably guided by a wiser curation, while not immersed

and lost in the mess of the crowd. I don't mean that one should retreat to absolute quietude or never challenge one's conceptions. Indeed, instead, you can always rethink things and interrogate yourself and your ideas and the wider world, and doing this does not require a full immersion into undiplomatic and abusive discourse which can instead be observed at a safe distance. One doesn't need to *talk* online with extremists to know them. I have become adept at observing the worst people, silently lurking in their spaces, a ghost they'll never see collecting a record of their follies.

It is possible to read and comprehend opposing ideas without getting involved in a venomous argument with an uncharitable interlocutor. Sometimes it is required; for the sake of safety and avoiding abuse. This idea is forgotten in online spaces, where the pressure to be *engaged* is so encouraged, regardless of any tact or responsibility, regardless of whether you know anything or not, and disengagement is considered rude or cowardly instead of healthy or respectful of one's limited resources.

Most arguments aren't sober: one is derailed and consumed by passion and emotion that is hard to direct usefully or efficiently. The faraway observation of foreign arguments can be more beneficial than being involved, just as a mountain can be better perceived for its true magnitude from afar, rather than with one's face in the dirt. I won't discount the possible utility of being closely involved in slanderous debate, and I'll even insist that regional and local knowledge, intimately involved, is vital for any bigger picture to ring true—but I'll contend that fully formed and cogent ideas are made best at a safer distance with the time and ability to reflect and review. At least for me, and at least if one doesn't have the time.

"Are most of our readings of theory not shoddy, as we pin down labels and allegiances? We name what we do not understand."

In June 2021, President Emmanuel Macron was slapped by a member of the public, a medieval combat enthusiast. Views varied on whether it was a deliberate, premeditated act of violence or an act of impulse. Investigating the background and the politics of the attacker, Damien Tarel, his beliefs were described as 'ideological mush'. This is easy to say when it's obvious, when someone's views are a hodgepodge of different influences and motivating violence. My reaction was almost snobbish. Most people are 'ideological mush'. Who isn't? It's funny when people think they aren't mushy.

People attest to or try to conceptualise others as having, somehow, a more or less consistent set of beliefs, especially when they are powerful, when a great majority of people are instead caught well within 'the muddledness of thought', or an otherwise vague sets of ideas, good, bad, everything in between, understood well or not, that are cobbled together as if they're impulsive consumers picking curious items from the store aisle. Consistent beliefs that could be easily described as monolithic, or non-hypocritical political or philosophical ideas are rare, or primitive and terroristic. In part, one wants some sort of diverse mixture of ideas—but the contention is how well-rounded and well-understood any regularly employed concepts and vocabulary are.

Popular pundits, filling the space of more humble intellectuals, more adept at carousing, looking attractive, better bullshitters, and better at advertising their wares, only have vague understandings of a variety of things they mush together. Some of those understandings are more lucid than others, while some are completely erroneous. William James warned of a professionalisation of academic and scholarly discipline that would distance truly learned thinkers from public spaces or make them less adept in public spaces than con-men, grifters, sophists, and others more capable, more hubristic, and less cautious than responsible thinkers. The arrogance of some professional academics, scoffing at the idea of public engagement or activism, further distances them from the public and laypeople—who then have their curiosities satiated by others far less responsible or knowledgeable. Forever a pessimist, I'd say James' warnings weren't heeded.

Few people have a real idea of how to properly define concepts and allegiances, misusing and misunderstanding all the usual and most common political vocabulary, all loaded with obnoxious connotations; some of them will have beliefs that are better constructed or more of a social conscience than others, but most are never going to be *that* thought out, and for anyone who does want some level of deeper and broader thinking or reflection, what they have most availably at hand is the great variety of modern punditry and not very many who are serious thinkers.

This doesn't mean I'm being sanctimonious, or admonishing everyone and saying they are stupid. Smarter people understand ideas and events and will still be limited by preconceptions and experiences, or the narrowness of their expertise, and we lie if we say we are truly, and so often, coherent and acute in our understanding.

Believing in a sense of ideological consistency, or consistency of ideas that aren't so much ideological, becomes dubious when very average people, or even most people, will, say, hold beliefs reaching in all sorts of directions—where on one hand they can be pro-choice and against abortion restrictions, but also equally believe that all of #MeToo was a nefarious plot to discredit one's favourite actor.

Here's another subject that's been done to death, but I'll state it for the record regardless: given how technology and media have changed culture, if I'm being crude, the terms *public* and *intellectual* are often far apart. What's more common are people who are very public: pundits, clickbait YouTube video essayists, think tanks, networking accounts, newspaper columnists, who to some degree may

be smarter than others (and may hold something valuable) but are often very much not serious theorists (though many will think they are). Serious intellectuals still definitely exist outside the ivory tower, and definitely should, but many are restricted, professionalised, and do not have the same proportional public reach as past figures during the 19th and 20th centuries, where a different relationship between media, technology, and culture meant they could be afforded a different stage. There is no direct analogue in the 21st century, someone of the same level of both fame and expertise, to Jean-Paul Sartre or Andre Malraux, or Isaiah Berlin, in the public space—regardless of how right or wrong they were on things. Public intellectuals today are, in simplistic terms, afforded less fame and celebrity than in previous decades; and that public space is instead filled by those with less ability or creativity.

This doesn't suggest the past was any better, but rather that people of the same intellectual weight and also the same public weight, with both real knowledge *and* fame, had an easier time existing in the past; whereas now, crudely, fame is easy but real knowledge is not. I won't be rude as there certainly are some YouTubers with intellectual weight—it'd be wrong to be so derogatory or elitist—and authors, teachers etc. can still maintain something of a public presence, but the process of culture and technology has done more to proliferate terribly noisy pundits and sophists, less so anyone with real brains. It is easier to find 'science explainers' or people with deep, yet narrow expertise explaining to a common audience difficult scientific concepts as pop intellectuals, but philosophers, historians, sociologists etc., with real quality are drowned out by noisy punditry in a way they weren't, at least so easily, in the past—with all the past's many faults—due to the internet, the easier availability for anyone to say anything publicly, and due to media democratisation.

I could argue against what I've just said: that extremism, fascism, and genocide still occurred during an idealised age of *men of letters*, and the expansion of right-wing fanaticism and anti-democratic tendencies is extant whether it's in the mess of today's media or the limited media of the past. So what's the use of nostalgically yearning for better public intellectuals? As a pessimist, again, I'll complain and say maybe it's more difficult now given the quantity of voices. If we were alienated in the past, how about now?

In more basic terms, if you ask an average person to name a public intellectual today, they will name someone public, but not someone intellectual. If you asked someone this question before the 1990s, chances are they'd more easily name someone with both qualities.

People who are, quote: 'real intellectuals' who are also known public personas still exist. Charles Taylor in Canada (though he's about 91 now), John Gray in the U.K., professors like Timothy Snyder, who has both an imagination and a social conscience (which can be rare), and acts partly as an activist and also a serious intellect with real credentials and quality.

There are otherwise 'intellectual entertainers' who will have a good thing to say or possess some real brilliance, in some capacity, but are still closer to 'populist intellects' rather than critical scholars.

Who am I to say all this? I'm just a boy and a fool and I'm certainly not very well qualified. I don't have a serious academic understanding of many, many things. I'm far closer to tedious and noisy talking-heads than I am to serious scholarship.

I don't mean to be so sanctimonious. Those with a lack of expertise can still reflect and parrot what's been said by greater minds, and someone lacking rigour and real schooling can still say stuff that is essentially just and correct—and sometimes more so, with more of a social awareness and moral consciousness than cloistered academics. Being smart doesn't always mean having good judgement.

The wish, sent out into the world with little hope of any change, is for more humble, responsible, and insightful people to have an improved standing in public affairs. I've said before, grimly, that we get the intellectuals and celebrities we deserve. If they aren't very good or very smart, that might reflect on us. I'd hope we could do better.

P art of me wants to forget the unforgettable. Unlike many (at least evidenced by their behaviour), I can't be blithe and forgetful about the pandemic, minimise its impact, equivocate on its wider implications or deny inconvenient truths, as I'd do so at a greater risk than others. Still, the cost of any awareness I have of painful realities and unfortunate events, the result of any 'doom-scrolling' as it is colloquially known, even of accounts I'd know to be cogent and devoid of any tabloid sensationalism, is emotional destitution and depression. I have to retreat from bad news and can't be some active force, as it ruins me: emotionally, physically; it wrecks me and leaves me unable to do anything while I remain the whole time, anyway, most of the time, in my own home away from the world. I have to retreat and manage risks and the primary way I do this is simply by staying at home, not going out, even if others wished I might be less worried about everything—or if everything outside was less worrisome.

I can complain and moralise as much as I want; I could, if I really had the heart for it, reprimand anyone close to me who has anything to do with me for causal and passive, everyday behaviour that could possibly open me to harm, like a stingy, pedantic moralist condemning everyone for their unconscious contributions to harm. *No ethical consumption, no ethical reciprocity.* But I'm not well-disposed to destroying all my relationships by calling every person I know a eugenicist for their milder infractions: which is also not a helpful way of changing behaviour. And I'd sound a bit silly. It's not effective.

There's little I can do unless others improve their behaviour, or improve their policy. I'm too tired and ineffectual to be some sort of activist or moraliser, and I don't have any political influence to change laws or culture. How we historically dealt with cholera and legionella is by improving infrastructure and by public effort. Instead, with Covid, we indulge in the lie of personal choice—which means the choices of a majority to ruin other lives considered less important. There could be improvements to infrastructure: with ventilation, air purifiers, and more that could mitigate Covid—just as we have long-standing public health protections against the aforementioned cholera and other diseases. One occasionally sees quiet implementations of this infrastructure, though normally reserved for the rich—while anyone else is free to harm or appears to care less. People are more willing to protect against venereal diseases, less so respiratory ones—even if respiratory diseases spread more easily. The politicisation of basic health measures, its own contentious and storied affair one could devote volumes to, means this appears like a lost fight. Especially if one doesn't have the stamina to keep up.

Unfortunately, it is the greater will of the public to passively and easily get on with their lives and not make sacrifices or investments to protect others (and protect disabled people, especially). For them, it is easier to peaceably carry on with everyday activities and not change. If the cost of this action, or inaction, is mass disablement (and much more), they don't appear to care very much or it doesn't cross their minds. People find any reason to justify their lack of care, or they just ignore things. The risks of the pandemic are minimised, equivocated, rationalised, denied, or ignored before being faced with what real implications they bring. It means I and others like me have to be vigilant and make our own sacrifices, while others don't care if we die or if we are all infected with a particularly pernicious, yet preventable contagion over and over again. They might say they care, but they won't act. And all I'm doing here is venting.

Camus had a quote: "Stupidity has a knack of getting its way." It is easier to be stupid. It takes less thought and time, you don't have to be so careful, you can afford to be forgetful, and life doesn't seem as hard if you are stupid. Stupid ideas and stupid actions will proliferate and spread more easily than better ideas. Or, if we are more charitable: it's easier to be ignorant and get on with life in peace, along the path of least resistance, than do something mildly inconvenient.

It might be easier to incentivise behaviour with policy, as moralising won't work, but there's little sign of policymakers doing that unless nihilistic financiers become more explicitly concerned with the loss of working human capital to increasing disability. Others will deny life to the grave.

Eugenics, from its tamer and indifferent iterations up to its most explicit and actively violent variants, is present through the perceived left, centre, and right of many politics. Real concern for disabled lives is harder to find than we'd wish or otherwise commonly believe. Others think their political or philosophical adherences mean that of course they're on the correct side of history and morality, advocating for the needs of the oppressed—yet they're often inconsistent, myopic, and engage in the above behaviour anyway, and more dishonestly. If one thinks one's truths are *obviously true*, axiomatically true, historically inevitable, rather than true and with robust defence, it's typical to encounter dishonesty and endless rationalisations of falsehoods. Encountering an honest racist or an honest eugenicist is almost a relief insofar that one knows exactly where they stand, while others keep pretending they're virtuous or somehow sincerely believe in their good fight while they dismiss, deny, or fail to consider disability—and much else.

I don't want to harbour some aggrieved victim complex, but can I help that? It's still true, given the evidence and regular reminders, that disability and ill health, through most cultures, is regarded as revolting, disgusting, a morbid existential reminder, or otherwise undervalued when juxtaposed with healthier lives. I don't want to be so preoccupied with this anymore, but it's inescapable and I don't have much optimism about altering it. My life is risk mitigation, not progress.

I have to retreat and hope I'm lucky enough to escape things.

The quotidian revulsion, disgust, or mockery of disability hasn't reformed much since FDR had to make such a logistical effort to hide his disability from public view. There are legal progressions, representational progressions, and maybe in some spheres a moral progression where at least some now don't view sickness and disability as sinful and immoral. Stating this to non-disabled people, of many persuasions, often motivates them to feebly grasp at an idea of better principles: that we truly have progressed, that things are better . . . It takes very little evidence to disabuse one of this optimism, with even minor research into medical neglect, public humiliations, pervasive and common attitudes, and legal dead-ends. Both medicalised and socialised views on disabled life are not so morally improved. The 'optics' of disability, the consideration of how it will appear to casual observers, are still almost entirely negative or pitiable.

Donald Trump, always one to project a vain image, was only persuaded to receive real Covid treatment, once he tested positive, after being informed that if he waited too long he'd no longer be able to walk to his car or helicopter, but would need to use a wheelchair—which would look pathetic and weak. We couldn't have that.

Disabled people often feel a sense of political and social homelessness. They aren't accepted in reactionary communities with more overt ideas of a 'might is right' social order; it's difficult to find acceptance in many more progressive communities, whether they're perceptibly centrist, liberal, of the left, or anywhere else, as somehow disability is a subject where even the smartest of people remain grossly ignorant. It's hardly the fundamental philosophies and ideologies, which will be bad enough, but the blithe and causal, passive and everyday actions—the easygoing dismissal where it wouldn't even cross one's mind to consider this dimension. Activists hope, some sincerely and earnestly, others in desperation, that things may become better. In marketing these concerns, appearing far too morose and defeated isn't effective. But we don't have to go far to recognise a great sense of hopeless resignation to a world that will never accept us, where the animal fear of sickness and death reflects a wider, implicit refusal to ever consider us equal persons, in each utilitarian scenario or appeal to deontological worth.

I don't want to appear heroic, or saintly, and I am always wary of receding into a traumatised victimhood offering no escape or respite. Self-flagellation isn't helpful, and aggressive indignation fails to persuade many of anything but further alienation and hostility. I am endlessly critical of both poles of righteous activism and polite society for ineffectively coping with structural issues, or ideological, teleological, pedagogical or personal issues. I don't want to be hopeless while surrounded by everyone's failure.

My only attempt is an intimate appeal, to those I know, to those with whom I have some currency, to make some small effort towards a world that isn't so cruel.

Alina Stefanescu

Arguments With Ibsen Concerning the Final Opus (or Finale)

ON FERNS

If disgust is a form of attention, you have mine. All three front porch ferns froze stiff last night, the trinity aiming towards that brownish-green hue that blurs the line between freezing and burning. To freeze or to fry: both endings may feel the same to a fern. We have the emotional extremism of ferns in common, you and I—you being Henrik Ibsen, Norwegian dramatist whose last play, *When We Dead Awaken*, was written in 1899; I being one who doesn't believe in accidents.

ON TITLING

Originally, you named the play *The Resurrection Day* after the sculpture buried inside it. I prefer this original title. A limpid misogyny occurs when an artist removes words from the mouth of his mistress and titles the play accordingly.

Irene said "When we dead awaken, we find that we have never lived," but you know what she meant. You know she was always alive, and not even your play could kill her. In changing the title, you changed the direction in which the play would be reviewed. When the dead awaken, Andrew Katzenstein will still be mourning a woman's decision to pose nude for a sculptor as a *sacrifice*. Katzenstein will mourn this publicly in major literary publications. I will read him with an eye to the product, or the procession of virtues men have come to expect from the stage.

After a day spent wrangling small mammals through this exceptionalist American childhood, I'd be enthused to pose nude for a dinoflagellate—and I would do this for nothing, by which I mean twelve hours of sitting naked on a stool with no responsibility apart from breathing.

ON FEMALE BODIES AS VIRTUE SIGNALS

I get it. Idleness makes a woman seem clueless, consumable, submerged in the sort of silence a man feels compelled to explain—but you know the part you didn't write, Henrik, how Irene enjoyed wandering through the forest the sculptor's eyes made of her; the way he created her in private knowing others could never see what he saw in public, knowing with every motion that his art could neither make her nor hold her. It was the only time she got a break from being interpreted. We love it when you create us, Henrik. It's your story then. You love us for sitting and hate us for enjoying it. 1899 was gammy for women. To be exalted in a world of few avenues, Henrik, is hardly the end of a life. 2021 has offered women the occasion of uplift through pandemic: we write books, work for money, and virtual school our children. Let us hope that someone is being paid for the labor of your pleasure.

ON THE SCULPTOR

I feel for him; the sculptor's sorrow is mine. It hurts to know that the public's admiration of *The Resurrection* is the beautiful lie that hides their fascination with Irene, the model who brought him fame. It's easy to envy the subject. Easy to disparage Irene's role by calling their time together an *episode*, thus narrowing its relevance to a particular duration. But you and I know a fern's feelings influence its shape; an episode develops, causes growth, thickens the frond. Even birth, itself, is episodic, the first event between fragments of significance, the beginning must signify the instant that informs a life. I have come to suspect: everything happens. Everything hurts. Everything happens to hurt.

ON SUBJECT-OBJECT CORRELATIVES

But you're a dick for dying before acknowledging what you did to Irene. There you are, stranded atop the Mountain of Eternal Great Moroseness for abandoning her in the gaudiness of muse-trope. That is no way to treat the love of your life, or even an episode. The play is dominated by images of stone and petrification. Why not let Irene be Irene for a moment?

Irene never accused the sculptor of ruining her life. She never *actually* said: ". . . you thoughtlessly took a warm-blooded body, a young human life, and ripped the soul from it—because you needed to create a work of art."

Just as she never blamed him for the death she chose by living the wildest life, that series of husbands, lovers, landscapes. The time has come. The bell has donged. Admit that it was you and not Irene who said those things, Henrik. It was you who killed her. Like I killed my ferns— by the accident I don't believe in.

ON FORGIVENESS, RECONCILIATION, AND INDUSTRIAL HOPE

Because I love you with the wantonness reserved for ferns, papier mâché ponies, and platforms of failed moral edifice, I will clean up the mess you left by dying right after this manuscript, Henrik. I will use my son's boomerang to organize my thoughts into something solid, a clavicle. Of course Irene was furious with the sculptor for killing his masterpiece, for severing its connection to the subject that gave it life. It is both folly and weakness to rip the electrical cord from the leafblower and then complain about the leaves. The sculptor was a coward whose cowardice was so baroque that it overpowered his relationship to art. Having nothing baroque to lose, Irene indicts him for that disappointment, for that level of bovine bathos. What is less interesting than offering one's body to a man who can't enjoy possessing it?

ON YOUR SILENCE (AND MINE)

I've been quite silent. Today, I made three turkey sandwiches and kissed the meat before laying it on an unbreakable plate before my children. The ferns are not silent. They are too dead for that. The ferns want to know Henrik, who you tried to address in what critics called this "piece of self-caricature."

My mother required us to resolve any fight before going to sleep . . . in case we died in our beds with that malefice between us. She said that peaceful sleep needed peaceful minds, but I knew what she meant. I haven't forgotten her unshaved armpits. Nor have I forgotten the other things I knew as a child, despite maturing to understand the politeness of bringing these regular childhood atrocities into adult conversation. All nuance is Instagrammed now. Of course my mother died in her sleep in Amsterdam, a city I cannot forgive.

ON STAGED SILENCE

This you do well. I felt nurtured and beloved in the silence between train stations: that blank the sculptor calls home. It is true that: "There are always two men, walking up and down, and talking—". There is always a story in what these men want from the world with their words, their boots, their bold lanterns.

OTHER SILENCES

Adrienne Rich mentioned them.

ON THE LITTLE CHE IN EACH OF US

Another brilliance: the sympathy you create for the sculptor. When he titled his masterpiece, "The Resurrection Day," the public misunderstood—they loaded it with something that was never in his mind. The revenge was partly sweet, enacted in his marriage to the cute, artless Maia, nourished through an obsession with wealth and finery, continued as a sabotage of his own art. I imagine the sculptor working on commission, making those busts to adorn wealthy homes, burying domestic animals inside the heads and faces—the thrill of his secret destruction. There is a Che Guevara in each of us. And only one way to betray the masterpiece of anything, really, that bitterness through which we let the world in.

ON PIN-UPS AND NUNS AND 90'S GOTH BANDS

The Sister of Mercy is sexy, Henrik. A writer who infuses the script with unrepentant nun sexuality must be prepared for the way she undermines it. The Sister of Mercy is a pin-up who lacks walls on which to be hung. This is awkward. It puts the reader in the position of simultaneously wanting to see and ignore a Sister. It put me, personally, in the position of penitence, wanting to feel something broader than pity for the stranger who has rented the little pavilion and left us with no further tease.

I liked being teased. I like fainting on purpose but only in secret. Not so for Katzenstein the critic, whose pleasure hinges on intimacy with adverbs. He is too majestic for evidence, including the bit when the sculptor tells his wife: "I have in reality had only one single model. One and only one—for everything I have done."

Poppycock loves company, I tell the neighbor whose cat often naps on our porch. The cat's Christian name is Poppycock. When a man resorts to sentimental hyperbole, why can't we believe him?

ON FERNS WHO RISE FROM THE DEAD

The resurrection fern is also known as *Pleopeltis polypodioides.* According to experts, this particular creature can lose 97 percent of its water content without dying. During drought, it shrivels into a gray-brown stirrup of leaves. It does not speak, move, or make dinner; its entire being waits for water to return. And when water returns, the fern resurrects, which is to say, it looks green, healthy, vibrant, the things we expect of life. The fern comes back to life without ever dying. The fern, Henrik, was never actually dead.

I know this much, Henrik: he won a piano competition with a piece composed by staring at a photo of me, and putting my name in the title. A piece to which I was titular. A piece he wrapped round my neck like a feathered boa. A piece he claimed to compose from a photo of me smiling in the snow. At him. Like the world had ended because it snowed in Alabama and I smiled in the frozen wetness. It was my first episode. And nothing stung like the discovery that, decades later, the piece was printed under a different title. Nothing hurt like the sound of him taking his gaze away from me.

Wilting usually reflects part of the dying process for a plant. I suspect the resurrection fern does not wilt: it simply exists in what resembles a wilted fetal position, or what might be a fetus in plant-based conditions. And maybe he lied. Maybe the piece had nothing to do with me at all. Maybe he composed it after a particularly compelling session with a porn magazine and his fist. That is my favorite daydream: idyllic along the edges.

ON BEAR-HUNTING MASCULINITY, BRAWN, AND MANLY WHITE STALLIONS

Henrik, your bear-hunter is what we of the 21st century might call *peak maudlin* when using adjectives to bolster a male whose brutality nears the banality of college football games. Late-stage capitalist machismo is very mod. The bear-hunter serves the purpose of mocking masculinity. The bear-hunter appears to be an early adopter of late-stage capitalism's Jedi mind-tricks. The bear-hunter is brilliant in his description of the Sister as "someone on the point of giving up the ghost." This makes the Sister of Mercy sound like a grave-robber pin-up, a late-consumerist lure for the apocaylpso.

The author of *When We Dead Awaken* resembles the man who feels guilty about his lover's abortion and then asks another woman (whose name may be Irene) to carry the weight of wanting a child to die so he can bury the relief of not having to say it himself. This is a common tactic in anti-choice pamphlets—the male wears the laurels of grief while the female gets moral credit for murder.

Was Irene ever as beautiful when she said she should have killed that child, the life that minimized her own, the birth that cast her existence into footnotes?

Look. A mother's heart is heavy with love's survival. A mother's heart is lightened by the children she kills, the ones that never grow to become statues. Does the author feel similarly about his books?

ON THE MAIA'S WHO ARE DRAFTED FOR WHITE STALLIONS TO SAVE

"In the foreground on the right a hillock"—and Maia with her giddy cuteness; Maia, who needs to believe that painting a nude means something. Dear Henrik, I blame you for upsetting Andrew Katzenstein and muddling poor Maia's head with americanist theories, including the idea that posing naked must take something from a woman by automation, an automatic thought, a gentlemanly assumption, a need for a white stallion to enter the story. You do nothing to dissuade us from believing that the physical exposure is what hurts Irene, that the surface of the lake is the story of the life beneath it.

I blame you the way I don't blame the man in the original episode. His lie, unlike yours, remains fascinating. Or which lie—the one he told to me, the one he told to the world, the one he told to himself, the margins in which these lies taste different?

I know this: Led Zeppelin undercut by the aroma of Irish Spring. And whatever it takes to make me sit still and look at you, again. Atoning. Atonement. The familiar costume of guilt worn for serving—in service of being adored.

ON RODIN

The man in the original episode went to Paris with me. We visited Auguste Rodin's museum. I probably wrote a sonnet about it invoking Rilke. At no point did I not consider the affair between Rodin and Camille Claudel, his student and co-worker, to be "dark". I did not consider darkness in the context of so much creative marvel, fever, light.

Rumor has it you were trying to tell Rodin and Claudel's story, but I think most rumors are lies. Usually the truth is personal, nearer to the hip. Maybe the truth is the cool lip of a lie I haven't told yet. The truth is waiting. My eyes rise to touch each word as it settles on his face, the ice-pick anticipation.

ON FLEAS, MONKS, AND MEN

In the 14th century, good wives kept fleas from the marital bed by placing a glue-slathered slice of bread with a candle in the middle as a trap. We assume the fleas sought the flame. We create traps to catch each other according to what we believe is desirable. We define ourselves by what desires us. Monks saw personal vermin like lice as a mark of piety, evidence of active self-mortification. A linchpin to martyrdom, wearing the hairshirt, its wool thick with fleas. The torture of the marathon runner. Sisters of Mercy didn't have to indulge as much physical self-flagellation. It seems menstrual cycles were deemed brutal enough.

"Those two choices which a woman has—to be less than a woman or less than a person—are highly painful," said Robin Lakoff. I am sharing this quote from my notebook because I know you understand choices are painful for women, for fleas, for monks, for men, especially male deities.

Consider the view from here, as I understand it, as the retired lawyer shoots the heroin straight into his vein while his wife sweeps broken glass from the porch. A child abandons her pink bike on the front lawn. A boy carries a broken kite beneath his favorite arm. A woman lowers her head between the thighs of a man who is not her husband or even her mailman. A man uses the word love like frozen dinner. All these things happen in the mind of God in one moment.

ON INCOHERENCE, STAGECRAFT, DEATH

As for the playwright, all the things in his mind will happen on stage. Irene was fine with being naked, vulnerable, sculpted, exposed to human eyes. What Irene couldn't survive was the writer: the man who couldn't take her off the pedestal of purity and innocence long enough to touch her. See Henrik, it's not that he used her—it's that *he didn't*. It's that his gaze transformed her into a "thing hallowed . . . not to be touched save in adoring thoughts." What a horrible thing to say of a thing. What puerile objectification.

". . . if I desired you with my senses, my soul would be profaned . . ." Dear God, the sculptor would have been a fantastic emcee for a purity ball. I'm sorry he missed out on the future.

"I fashioned her in your image, Irene," is an excellent sort of thing to say to ferns, a godly discourse that acknowledges the effect of pollution on the water we feed them. An early-stage eco-terrorism.

"Why can we not do what we will?" Irene asks the sculptor on the mountain, or in its shadow. I, too, have asked this of men in bars and parks. I have asked this of Confederate monuments. I find the stone speaks more than the flesh, though I am no sculptor; I find the stone, at least, has a plan.

Where the sculptor can't decide what he wants from the sculpture, or from Irene—if she is a prodigal, a portrait of purity, a glorification, an insensate mass . . .

Some of the things Irene says are so incoherent that I suspect you of drinking, Henrik. Or staring too long at bobbing swans.

There is a moment of clarity when the sculptor expresses his need for a partner to be one with him —to be one with him and all his "striving"—to adopt his striving as her own, as one might expect from a fan or else a distraction that might lure him away from the bitterness of making art for fame, making art in order to be seen. This is the Che Guevara moment. This is the point at which the woman is returned to the pedestal where she can provide to man's moral needs.

I think many of us would pose nude and feel nothing. I think many of us have, and will continue to do so. I think it's less exciting than riding a swan into a magic forest and building a nest with no god's name looming in the corona to blame us. The dead are too tired to wake and do dishes.

ALL PROGRESS BEGINS WITH DEVIANCE.

Kurt Luchs

The Mystery of Gabriela Mistral

Actually, there are several mysteries surrounding Gabriela Mistral. Which is odd, given that she was the first Latin American author and one of the first women to receive a Nobel Prize for Literature (1945). Her work is known and loved throughout the Spanish-speaking world, particularly in her own country, Chile. Yet she remains very little heard of in English. In our current age you would think doctoral candidates would be falling over themselves to write dissertations on this groundbreaking Hispanic woman writer who was almost certainly a lesbian (though she was so secretive about her emotional life that some slight mystery still lingers over that question).

The outward facts of her life are well established. She was born Lucila Godoy Alcayaga in Vicuña, Chile, on April 7, 1889, and died in Hempstead, New York, on January 10, 1957, at the age of 67. Her father abandoned the family when she was two years old, inflicting the first of several significant wounds by a man in her life. In 1906 she fell in love with a railroad worker, Romelio Ureta, who committed suicide for unrelated reasons in 1909. The next man she loved married another woman and broke Lucila's heart. She was deeply hurt, but strong. She

had been supporting herself and her mother since the age of 15, working as a teacher's aid in Compañia Baja, a coastal town. By 1904 she was already writing and publishing poems in local newspapers under various pseudonyms, beginning a lifelong habit of guarding her privacy. Ten years later, in 1914, she won a national literary competition with her "Sonnets on Death" (Sonetas de la muerta). These poems responded to the death of her first lover, the death of love itself, and perhaps also the death of her father, who passed away in 1911 still estranged from his family.

The literary prize was a turning point. From that time on, with few exceptions, she adopted the pen name by which she is still known. Depending on which version of the story you prefer to believe, she took "Gabriela" either from Italian writer Gabriele D'Annunzio or the angel Gabriel, and she took "Mistral" either from Nobel-winning French poet Frédéric Mistral or the mistral wind so common in Provence. The pseudonym was at least partly motivated by fear of losing her job if her employers became aware of her unusually frank and disturbing poems. Her fame as an educator was growing as rapidly as her literary renown. Teaching jobs in country and coastal towns gave way to a position in the Department of Education in the capital, Santiago. This led to her being headhunted by the Mexican Minister of Education to help reform his country's system of education in 1922. She was only 33. Extraordinary!

Meanwhile she continued to publish poems, prose poems, fables, stories and essays on a multitude of topics, including the rights of women and children. Though she clearly needed to express herself and wanted her work to be known, she seemed curiously indifferent to putting out a book, another mysterious lifetime quirk. And in fact her first book was not her idea and wasn't even published in her own country originally. "Desolacion" (1922) came about because a Professor of Spanish Literature at New York's Columbia University, Federico de Onis, had taught her poetry to his students. Her work bowled them over, and when they learned she had no book as of yet, they assembled one themselves and published it through the university's imprint.

Mistral would deserve a place in the history of literature if only for her friendship with and her encouraging and mentoring of the young Pablo Neruda, 15 years her junior. The parallels between their careers are worth recounting. Not only do they share the honor of having received a Nobel Prize. Each of them won that prize for a body of work that included poems written when they were mere teenagers, poems that made them instantly famous. Neruda and Mistral shared a preference for writing under a pseudonym. They also shared a devotion to social justice, pursued by Neruda through the communist party politics of his day, and by Mistral through her more independent path, which, it is fair to say, did more actual good. Finally, they shared in benefitting from Chile's enlightened policy of letting its writers and artists serve in a consular capacity throughout the world. (Would that the United States were half as civilized!)

The poem we're looking at here, "La Lluvia Lenta" ("Slow Rain"), was written in 1914 when the poet was 25 and became part of her first book, "Desolacion", in the section called "Naturaleza" ("Nature"). The first English translation was by H. R. Hays. It appeared in Poetry magazine in May 1943 in an issue devoted to Latin American poets. That same year Hays, one of the finest translators of Hispanic poetry, assembled an anthology called "12 Spanish American Poets", which did much to bring the best writers of the region to the awareness of North Americans. Early translations of Borges, Guillen, Vallejo and Mistral's own student Neruda are there—but not Mistral herself. In fact there are no women poets at all! To me this is a shocking omission, especially given that Hays knew her work and admired it enough to translate it for Poetry. Chalk up another Mistral mystery.

In the original Spanish, the poem consists of eight stanzas. Each stanza begins with three octosyllabic lines and ends with a tetrasyllabic line (i.e., four syllables, half as many). When I say the lines have eight syllables and four syllables, I am counting not the grammatical syllables, which are sometimes more or less than that, but the poetical syllables, the stressed ones. Does that make sense? Anyway, that's how they do prosody in Latin America, so the experts tell me. The second and fourth lines rhyme. Spanish being a much more rhyme-rich language than English, it is no doubt wise of Hays not to attempt a rhyming translation. Most of the rhyming translations that I've seen of Mistral's work in old anthologies are stilted and convey little of the music of the originals.

Hays manages to bring quite a lot of that music into English, using assonance and alliteration and a few other devices while keeping the structure. The first stanza establishes the direction and tone:

> This timorous, sorrowful water,
> Like a child that suffers,
> Before it touches the earth,
>   Falls fainting.

Water in general, as both symbol and fact, is a life-bringer. In a rural farming community like the one Mistral grew up in, it is everything. Without rain there will be draught, crops will fail, children will go hungry and farmers will sink even farther into poverty. Why isn't she celebrating the rain?

Perhaps because water is also a feminine symbol, and at this time in her life she quite rightly felt hindered, harassed and oppressed as a woman with a significant literary gift and a passion for teaching children who was banging her head against various walls. I don't know whether this poem was written before she won the national poetry prize that brought her first fame (both events occurred in 1914). But almost all of her triumphs were ahead of her, yet unknown. Among other things, the Catholic Church had denied her entrance into one of its teacher training schools because of her unorthodox writings, and she had to study for her teaching certificate on her own. This and similar happenings may partly explain the unrelenting sense of sadness and defeat in this poem.

Stanza two speaks of the "stupendous silence" in which "These clear and bitter tears / Keep falling." The well-worn trope of tears-as-rain gains power from the poem's (actually the translator's) first use of internal rhyme with "clear" and "tears". And now we can see that the poem is an extreme example of the pathetic fallacy, a projection of Mistral's deep suffering and grief onto the natural world. Stanza three makes it even more personal and painful, calling the sky "an immense heart / Which opens bitterly. / It does not rain: it is bleeding [. . .]" That is quite an imaginative leap, from rain to tears to blood, in such a short space. Women are fated to bleed every month, a blessing or a curse depending on who's doing the defining. Yet just as with the rain, the future of the human race utterly depends upon this difficult flow.

Just in case we missed the explicitly feminine aspect of this imagery, these metaphors, stanza four offers a stark contrast with another leading gender:

> Men indoors at the hearthstone
> Feel none of this bitterness,
> This gift of sorrowful water
>   From above us.

Stanza four is notable for several reasons. It cleverly, one might almost say satirically, identifies men, not women, as the real homebodies who hide indoors from the troubles of the world. Why do they not feel the bitterness of this slow rain? Because it is not woven into their very being as it is with women, who are part of nature, one with nature, in ways that men can never be (of course there are ways in which the opposite is also true, but they are not the focus of this poem). This stanza further affirms that the rain, while still sorrowful, is also a gift. What's more, a gift from "above us," i.e., god or the gods.

In stanza five we hear of "conquered waters" whose descent toward the earth is "wide and weary". The earth is described as "reclining / And exhausted." Rather late in the game, stanza six introduces the idea that the slow rain may be a dream:

> The lifeless water is falling
> As quietly as in a dream,
> Like the slight creations
>   Dreams are full of.

That's interesting. Does this suggestion of dreaming undercut what has come before or strengthen it? I think it does the latter. As we know, the seemingly "slight creations" of dreams often hold tremendous significance. At this time in her life, before she returned to the Catholic Church, Mistral was searching, questioning, and found an affinity for theosophy and Buddhism. This was also the period when she was most influenced by the modernist poets of Latin America, with their deep, complex symbology of images. The founder of *modernismo*, Rubén Darío of Nicaragua, was one of the early champions of Mistral's work before his death in 1916.

By far the most interesting thing about stanza six, however, is that Mistral later cut it from the poem. I have no idea why. In my opinion that edit was a mistake, but of course it's her poem, and anyone is free to read it both ways and decide for themselves, just as we can with the dueling versions of W. H. Auden's "In Memory of W. B. Yeats."

Stanza seven introduces another sharp turn in the narrative:

> [. . .] and like a tragic jackal
> Night lies in wait in the mountains.
> Out of the earth, in darkness,
>   What will rise up?

What indeed? Whatever it may be, it merits the second use of an internal rhyme by the translator, "tragic jackal". In this case, however, the rhyme does exist in the original. The implication of the imagery is vaguely but disturbingly ominous. Coming after the rest of the poem, I take it to refer to the thwarted gifts of womanhood, which, when deflected by a world run by men, do not lead to a happy conclusion.

The final stanza, number eight in the early uncut version of the poem we're looking at, continues the unwholesome water imagery: "And shall you sleep while, outside, / This sickly lifeless water of death / Is falling?" Undoubtedly, I feel, the poet asks this question of herself. The ending is thus a call for her to wake up. While it's impossible to get too specific an interpretation of all this morbid imagery, it's fair to take the final stanza as a call to action. The translator does his part to emphasize the conclusion by making this stanza only three lines in English, though it is four in the original Spanish. The poet, the dreamer of dreams, is the one challenging herself to make those dreams a reality. She knows she must be a conscious dreamer, one to heed both the call to creative vision and the call to train the minds of children, the two calls she pursued faithfully all her life.

Kurt Luchs

Wasted Years

I loved and hated a woman, but mostly loved.
She loved and hated me, but mostly hated.
When hope is gone its cousin, hopelessness, remains,
the ugly familiarity of which can be a kind of comfort.
I held a succession of meaningless jobs
made even more poignant because they enabled me
to pay for the privilege of being hated.
Clearly, I was not in my right mind.
The years crawled by like crippled dogs
trying to cross a major highway.
I couldn't write anything serious
as that would've killed me instantly.
Instead I wrote humor with heartbreak always
just beneath the surface, humor as a form of despair.
To make the time pass I read thousands of books,
which was like shooting myself in the head
with a nail gun firing the truths of others.
And then came the only good part
of every nightmare, the part where I wake up.

&

& my poems' subtexts honor sea otters, belly up, sighing,
O salty waters, whither our porpoise? If a swain's poems fall short
of their purpose, he had best install a finger in the beloved's nostril. (Either one.)

& the young surgeon shakes his fist at the dawn: "How dare you reveal
Granny Philomel's eczema! Roll backward into the night!"

& je t'adore sounds like shut the door. On what?
On whom? I doubt I'm the first to remark the confusion.

& an ingot dragged across a replica waterfall sounds like
squealing blackboard chalk. Further aperçu to follow.

& birds and trees mature and expire at velocities consistent
in their difference. We include mine shafts. In keeping
with the pace of more collegial times, battles should conclude with
a performance of Wellington's Victory, the shaking of hands
and popping of balloons.

& poetry should be more engaging than wallpaper.
Similarities spell trouble—not to disrespect walls or indeed paper,
which fall among legitimate interests. On an uneventful Wednesday,
 a poet rolls home in patterned lengths.

& as a test of authenticity, stand the applicant in sunlight
and look for signs of dissolution.

& depart through a windshield. Your faith will attend
to your wounds. If you must spit, do it on Ash Wednesday
and aim for my forehead.

& I find myself staring, perhaps at a ghost.
It's difficult to be sure with one's shirt pulled up
over one's face.

James Reidel

Five Poems

I-71

With low beams, we crossed the high
bridge over the Little Miami and then the
smack of southwestern Ohio was detected, of freshly mown grass rotting in
the median between the south- and
northbound lanes. You could pick out the
exact mile marker where the mold count
flexed, where you could lie a stuffed animal alongside the interstate. It tickled our
noses, like the out-of-town wedding
champagne that we left behind. And here,
in passing, was a good place to recite the
eleventh commandment of 14th Street,
Thou shalt not complain of the smell of sour milk,
as well as roll up the windows two buttons
at a time and go back to counting the white
lines, a tally to play with, to mentally nail
together into little stick crosses, more ppm
mined out of darkness just to stay awake.

13 Lines of Despair for Sanibel

Notes of coconut oil blow in the breeze
from the south as the tuck and roll of
bethonged moons and breast surgeries
ripple across the sugar sand—the sun
sinks into the Gulf— and my eyes devolve
to either side of my head like the lizards in
my regard of things to either side of me
(not wearing sensible sunglasses)—at least
the ingredients will read of sea salt in every one of my tears—and there was the
tarot of turning over sea grape leaves that
stick to my wet bare feet—and punching a

hole in one so as not to smart my eyes
much further staring directly into the
shadows the helmets make along the bike
paths—and thus spake the silence of the
snow crab unto the white birds: "Your
coral toenails shine—when my hands still
felt numb from falling through the flight
path that sucked the meat from my fingers"—and coming up from below were
"my black water shoes on point before
Madame Melanoma's barre"—hang on to
that title for a while—and the dragon flares
the full bore of his nostrils iced with SPF
50, yet his breath is no match for the hot
glue guns that hide behind every shell
shop souvenir—that here the nights are in
the come-in-threes, the ellipsis of Orion's
tan line—that every dash in every verse of
É. Dickinson is the lightning bolt I can
stitch together with just the accent stripes
down the line of cars jamming the cause-
way—that strikes a palm rat dead, picked
up by its tail, and seen from the air.

Indigo Children II

Then Dr. Bluespire leaned over his shoulder…

The only thing not here is the physi-
cian who lifts up the sheet to reveal
the soles of the feet, but the *Toe*day
show—I shall call it that from this day
on for the unseemly interest taken in
the blue toes of children taken to the
hospital. Anyone can see each little
piggy still has some white to it. Some
wiggle like worms on a hook. Were
Laius the President, and he was, in a
way once, as King of Thebes, he would
smack even the bluest toes with a
hammer and forge them into oedipal
toes. ("Edible, did you hear that, Ghis-

laine?") And just so you know why I would deign to pay attention to the television, it is that children are cruel, and God punishes them as well, because that is the one thing He does well. Kids sang "Tip Toe the Birthday Elf" whenever they saw me, when I, according to a man on a park bench, walked "like a faun"—this before I was fitted for my corrective shoes, for mortality. ". . . and we are seeing something else in ICU," said Dr. Voice Over to Ms. Pointy Head, this as I said good morning to her, backing away, backing into my shell across the hall. "It is a disturbing complication, a loss of concentration, that *might be permanent*"—but a blue glow! That anyone can see.

Hölderlin and Disappointment

Da ich ein Knabe war,
Rettet' ein Gott mich oft

Hölderlin thought long and hard about the gods and suffered what he believed to be their loneliness. He believed that they rescued each other from it or, to use another word with a more ominous note, their *neglect,* and that we should learn from their example. So, while everyone who knew better in his day pulled for Kant, Hölderlin could take the opposite Olympian direction as if by instinct. He retired to a tower. He was up there with the birds as many of his contemporaries observed, "a real weathercock of a fellow, clanging in the wind." But were we to take him seriously, pull for him as I do, suspend disbelief, the existence of the old gods, if one reads him right (as well as the copious secondary literature about him with even a modicum of apprehension), Hölderlin arrived on the most desirable form of fame vis-à-vis poetry: *the mortal acknowledgement of the immortal presence.* How does it work? How do you know a god exists, one in the room with you? Or walking by your side as a god does in one of Hölderlin's paeans to nature? When this poet was a child, he believed a god often came to rescue him from the vicissitudes of his 18th c. childhood, from adults screaming at him, caning him, and boxing his ears. This makes me think his first brush with fame was merely an imaginary friend in the modern sense, a "person" who can't even sign a baseball.

50TH

Circling above so as not to step in it, you can see tiny stars of down forming an outline, cottonwood seeds flocking around a pool in the reunion season, where we gather. But really! The June rains of yesterday must have blown under the flaps of the long tent staked in the student parking lot, one of those cloud pavilions with the plastic panes like looking through your tears. But there is still this strange attraction, to be circumspect. The "cotton" beards an island of water on the map and there is more than one puddle to step around, enough for us left, a beard like wisps of tissue corners staunching a regatta of shaving cuts. If you look straight down, you can ask your reflection to say something from the mirror in a white velvet frame, the beyond, or see something in the shape, lead pouring into the ruined face of our youth.

Four Poems

Trouble Every Day

after Claire Denis's film of the same name

Boys prove their randiness
by climbing up trellises
to get eaten. Béatrice D.,
the hungry one,
is also telluric
because her dark hair
neuters the gap
in her teeth, otherwise
a mark of lubricity
in nightjars
and the clinically post-verbal.
To Seth I lust primarily
after big noses.
But equally
I despise tendrils
whose cohesive office
exposure annuls.
For an integument
turned wispy
heralds the taillessness
of a show pony
and so
affirms pedigree's
mephitic eventuation.
As a non-transcendent
gesture
of bonhomie,
gurus in tweed
will harbor spiders, thereby
obviating the niftiness
of identificatory apps.

Not all leapers are deadly.
Consider brown portentous
if it dots the spinnerets.
What's your stance
on betrayal,
Mr. Brown?
Mme Cécile Inès
was elected ambassador
of the Disaffected
Cinematographers Guild.
She liaised with bigwigs
to combat the switch
to digital, citing
its amplitude
as a pox on film's
je ne sais quoi.
The execs rejoined
in kind: *Uvular,*
the contours
of fuzziness glamorize
light's fashioning
of skins human,
plant, and polyhedral
by pegging them
as styles.
Her efforts were
inconsequential
as topiary
or dandruff
on a nobody's shoulder.
Ip ip oorah
cheered those who'd
tired of aspiration.

Time Away in Athens

No, I don't want to come up.
The proposition sputtered in the city green.
Southwest of Syntagma,
plenty made do in the Acropolis cliffside.
      A trace of being buffeted.
      A team of Dutch archaeologists plotting
      the coordinates of a second,
      shiftier cemetery.
Marc's email elucidated a lot.
(His dance troupe announced their spring season;
he was considering corrective lenses;
he would never replicate the relationship.)
      I read Minoans liked
      to mat their hair but not,
      as with the Polish plait,
      apotropaically.
Not quite lost on Omirou
amid dazzlements
and pirate costumes.
Not yet seeing a cynocephalus,
      I thought to spit
      my dogtooth in the sink
      and grin like a naïf
      in the know.
As if aping the unnamed star
of an arthouse hit might clarify
the days ahead. Better to take the aorist
to heart: root an event without stopping it.
      Escorted by mutt to the club,
      I danced with Thanasis,
      full name Athanasios, "immortal"
      un-negated for a night of disco.

Everyone in a couple is either Carrie Coon
in *The Leftovers* or Carrie Coon
in *Gone Girl*, i.e., the debutante upstager
of Ben Affleck's rueful penis. Lately I've tried to inhere
in the hodiernal and keep my proprioceptive
apse uncluttered.
      For it was the summer
of gym rats and forsaken reconditeness.
The susurrus in the dark room—the darkness
a direct result of my failure: the poem,
though anagrammatic,
was not in the least angelological—
stemmed not from my hip flexors
nor from the owls
first figured in Termite Creek's
petroglyphs.
      Rather, I had progressed
from noting gladioli
to agglutinating the discs themselves—
heap and pull, heave and pearl, hie and release.
Never mind the stolid cutouts
whose imitability rendered base
the beaming concentricities.
      Upon swallowing
this capsule, anyone can savor a decade
condensed to a blippy reel on which,
for example,
Oleg's maturation into an Olympic disappointment
with eyes still mere as cornices luminesces
before putzing around.
      My project, then,
is one of substitution and citation, and its pretext
a stratum of infrangibility to which I resist
affixing any resolvable thrust. But to become
an It Girl, citation must acquire
supersedence such that
the It iteratively eclipses the nose
that sowed it. Mine's bulbous unoriginality
speaks for itself:

Put your love in me . . .
So resounded the armor
of the necrotic pangolin
when I was hoping for the singed wheat's
Skedaddle. My fervor bolsters
skimpy things: the scope of auteurist
self-imaging, a rodent's feed, itinerancy,
the boys' glitter shrub's steady inculpation.
          A fuddy-duddy activist
entrenched in the languor
of observational humor
may wish to defenestrate the limping duke
but with noblesse oblige settles
for a garden rake. And although he's raffish,
the groundskeeper eludes his sex's
nominality by committing to cataloguing
cinematic depictions of nunhood in crisis.
Go, figure.
          I chose to stock
a spice rack
to grasp the ins and outs of animacy
or, better still, life. I was a good sport.
I looked above me. Sooner than stars
I spotted their matrix, imageless
like a comparison.
          The lusciousness
of modular abutment is self-evident,
yet the linguist kept yapping about it
in various low-stakes situations:
a classroom game designed to teach
phonemic awareness, for one,
and the moment at the deli counter
when customers must choose
their schmear. He got in line
and merely looked the part
of a bagel devotee,
                    confirming
that temerity, like macramé, assumes
myriad shapes and styles.

Seated at a Distance from the Cool Lakes of Death

Jewish brothers living separately in Williamsburg
don't raise doves. Spurred by the remnants
of a misplaced Romanticism, they liked the idea
but couldn't stomach the obstreperousness
of the wan chicks' cooing. It was a nonissue.
Marketing professionals needn't keep birds
to justify use of "dovecote" over lunch
and at the occasional happy hour.
"Bats in the belfry" is another matter entirely.

<>

Max to me: I'm thinking of joining a juggling club.
Me to Jake: You should ring your brother's doorbell.
Norma Shearer to Athole Shearer: You'll never guess how my voice
    sounded!
Athole to me: A fishing rod before curving echoes the sip the roebuck
    took.
Max to Norma: Cantilevering the airplane will suspend its sense of duty
    but educe its star persona.
Jake to Max: Bess the Cow the corn snake prefers fancy rats.
The women to me: The difference between ancient and lasting is like
    that between décolletage
and dishabille, but you must think about it without recourse to
    thimbles, flowerpots, or smithing.
Me to the boys: Grab your dungarees—we're outta here.

<>

No one fords rivers anymore. Oh, some people
still do? That proves my point, and not in the Odysseus-Outis
vein of reasoning, which, though unctuously played out,
inspires a smirk every now and then. The story goes
that Odysseus, upon blinding Polyphemos, identified himself
as No One—*Ou Tis*—and so by dint of apophatic
guile and a pliable name escaped
Now No-Eyed's reprisal. It's de rigueur

to pity the Cyclops, and I do,
but not out of deference to popular opinion,
which the people are nevertheless welcome to
align me with, provided that any one of us has devised
a mechanism for concurrent self-extraction
and clear-eyed collective appraisal.
Anamnesis offers an enticing solution,
though the memory,
whose cosmopolitan scope one can't insure,
must be durational and purged
of funny business.

<>

As I rove, whether I sidestep the rowan berries
whose constitution as such the concrete reinterprets
depends on that day's tête-à-tête with light,
though studies have shown that clarity indices
can't detect photic attitude or a late-night pas de deux.
It snowed, and the housecats left
before the story ended. Freeways oughtn't mystify
but do. They're just asocial parallel determination.
Inalienable from the nature of a way is the notion
of an ocean, no, a priory of mollycoddled opals.
Everything's just. It's all mollycoddled.
The thought isn't that distant relations universalize us:
bookies are typically less dyspeptic than topiarists.
Instead, Thought sits naked at her time machine and winnows
while the night is long. Many will ask about the object.
There's so much fluttering here and there.

> THICKLY BUNDLED, STRAWS
> ARE UNBREAKABLE.

Six Poems

People Persons

You'll find out thirteen heroes prefer McDonald's fries and twelve believe in god. Then you see them one day, riding a cut top bus in Hollywood. A dozen Jesus hairdos sniffing the pissy wind. Dramamine stop at the gift shop to stuff the rising throw up. We're always saying of cities: It was nice today, not many people. Always pocketing competitions for our carry-ons; saying: I can't stand those second smaller signs advertising New York-style pizza.

Seasonal Ingredients

This weather hangs under your arms like a saber-toothed speech. A few times a day now I sit reading pages from my dog. Elementary days when she says sit and snails say go. Milk snails leaving ambition trails up the sliding glass door. If they're looking for a way in, they've found it. They've found the neon welcome sign of full spectrum light. The pilled blue pillow stuffing my oxbow spine. So somebody didn't wake up a bellwether for posture. So what? I'm doing mustard bread poultice snagging autumn burdock hooks. I've saved half a mind in the fridge to stitch a corset for my sandwich. My mash between two pillows. Give me a year, I'll get there.

Oh, you're home. That jet-bridge grand entrance was just the budge I needed. Now we're really sitting up a storm.

The Difference Between False Sense and Good Taste

What you must tell your
hotel about home. Your suitcase
about safety. Buttered thighs
about fake French lotions. Mornings
chugging strangled oat embryo.
Brand-name vitamins with better coating
than your neighbor's roof.
What you must tell ladders about chutes.

You must have told stained glass
it makes righteous bullets. Teeth,
they don't need a full set of president.
What you must have told
crooked horses about bullet trains.
Your spouse about satisfaction.

You don't always say it when you're shopping,
but fresh dill is such a nice surprise,
pinched in a baby gem salad,
alongside mushroom and onion flatbread.

Some People Resent Plastic Lemons

Who invented the blow-mold lemon?
Lazy polyethylene device,
whistles & sputters when clenched of its
last mist. There must be millions,
battered sunshine accordions,
floating Cornwall and Moloka´i gyres.

In my yard each season, one hundred
lemons lie there in disbelief that
something so precious is left to lie
there in disbelief. Until a friend
comes along to *tsk tsk tsk* the waste.
Gathers a bagful leaving one hundred
others for a billion feasting beings;
leaving enough jewels in the crown
for any friendly visitor. But,

considering the jif they've made of
citrus, I just dont know if I could
have over the inventors of the
blow-mold plastic lemon; though I'd love
for them to taste my real lemonade.
Damn it, they're probably really nice guys.

(According to various sources, the creators of blow mold plastic lemons, in
several iterations, were Edward Hack, Bill Pugh, and Stanley Wagner, circa
1940s-50s.)

Some People Go Without a Name

City neighbors name their white house *Bianca*.
Ours never had a name; at least call it *Farmette*.
Three dozen chickens and a dancehall of goats.
Two turkeys named after their expiration dates.
We didn't believe in god or luck, but
we swore to both when a limb landed too close.
Four of us still have ten fingers, so that's
one way to wave goodbye & toss out the trash.

What all those hits and misses could have named us.
Apparently, anything but *Persistence Pays Off*.

Dad had a name for that moment, that pre-
exhaustion, when he was about to cut
firewood for the stove that heated our house,
but would rather keep to the recliner
watching *Gold Fever*
with the black dachshund
petted pale like a bald restaurant Buddha:

"Awww, shit, shit, shit..."

Some People Are Called Crazy

Emil tallied every Sunday he'd seen a television.
Otherwise, acquaintances with bullfrog croaks.
Waiting for the rain to release its hold on
scrimping productivity. Anything rusty was a possibility.
Machine bolts salvaged from a Chrysler to splice dentures.
Chipped enamel basin to wash armpits with melted snow.
Burning the census for heat; when a hundred yards to the sauna
felt like frying pans strapped to frost-dead feet.

Emil tallied all the high-fallootin double-criss-crossers
coming to take him away. Bigwigs in swivel chairs,
out for his eighty acres and the tooth of a mule. Pellet gun boys
released on summer break. Out to scrimshaw his *Stay Away* signs.
Warning the crazy cat man that the future is coming.
How can you be crazy when you reach your eighties in the '80s?

With neon light glowing cataracts on your deathbed,
shy hush-hush of a radio in the hospital hallway,
you ask: *What's a Kajagoogoo?*

Six Poems

*

You are Harsh. I Stagger.
You Culminate in the Boundless.
I am your Pure Assassin.
You Dominate.
I Unite.
You Delegate.
I Endure.
You Occupy with Oppression.
I Capture your Imaginary Mischance.
You are the Epitome of the Ineffable, but your Miserable Destination is me.
You hide behind Mud Walls, to Drown out the Voice of the Informer,
so that I cannot Identify you, only Stimulate an Embrace.
In your Adjoining deception, I am your hired Contractor.
Are we both Clandestine enough, Inasmuch?
Your Crystalline soothes my Rectangular Negligence,
Inasmuch.

(in appreciation of Jorge Luis Borges)

Blueprint of a delusional fish-man

The blueprint prints a man from a manprint while delusionals fish for the man from a blueprint of his fingerprints while the fisherman wraps his steely blue gaze upon the man. The man of steel has stolen the blueprint of a man, a fingerprint of a fisherman from Hell, the brother of his sister's elbow, who conveys his delusions to the south side of Katmandu with more than enough postage to reach the virgin's knee. The virgin's original clamshell pastes its blueprint upon the face of a fish's pogo stick in the dim and distant future. But in the dim and near past, virginal slime falls to the feet of a fisherman who obfuscates the blueprints of delusion for all the sentinels and peoples of the world.

*

This stroll along the
street of wan dreams
brings things into
focus that
are better left blurry.

Blind trees reach out
to caress what they can't
see, and the face of the
river
laughs at their frustrations.

My hands are
powerless to stop the
sidewalk from retching
dead leaves into the air.

I am steps from the
door of my favorite cafe
but know I can't enter
because the river rushes
between me and the door.

I will be walking
down this street for
an undetermined time
until the face of the
river floats in my bed.

And when that time comes
the trees will gain sight
and dead leaves will spew
themselves through my door
and joy will finally arrive
as planned.

*

A vision of clouds woke you
on our last night together.
You took it as a frozen warning
that the patchwork Eden we
    invented,
that odd + even world of echoes,
no longer believed in you.

You blamed it on too much

dreaming of St. Catherine
and the decimation of souls
but those footsteps in the dark
each night,
under disfigured constellations,
were only your own.

My heart returns
to my woman in red
and the butterflies
under her skin,
and her lovelight in flight
and I still
believe in you.

*

In the nineteen-fifties
Baby, you were your own TV
under square light fixtures
and iceberg eyes
and the molten drip of your
    thoughts.

The wings of dawn
stole the lightening
from no one's little girl.

So you rowed a boat
to a place of forgotten fires
where you could consume
the most of what is least.

Come and stay with me
and remind yourself
of constellations and devotion.

*

In this fairy tale world of make
    believe
I strive to find a way out of the box
where grief and despair are
    unbreakable locks
in a world which only myself has
    conceived.

Stephen Kampa

Two Poems

The Human Factor

Postmodern muddle
means we drown
in signs

and scenes: dramatic
context acts

to frame the
face of
facts. A fact's

all affect
flecked with flux

and spin,
less checked than
checkered, often

chucked out windows,
even fucked—

one doubtful fact
projects doubt
on all facts'

effects, infects
the kicked stone's

arc till
all the body's
dark. Poor

facts, we miss
your taut

trajectories of thought.
How hard
to be consistent

or exact—
impossible, in fact.

Well, at Least They Got One Thing Right (Including 5.8% David Kirby, 3.1% William James, 2.4% Bad Ninja, 1.8% Andrew Marvell, .6% Lee Van Cleef, .6% Jocular Lexicographer, and .1% Shakespeare)

> *. . . and even these movies often have a scene*
> *or an exchange between two characters*
> *or a word said a certain way*
> *or maybe just a facial expression*
> *that you'll not only remember for years*
>
> *but use in a way that changes your life*
> *for the better . . .*
>
> —David Kirby

Okayokayokay, so Lee Van Cleef—*Lee Van Cleef*—
 turns out to be a ninja,
a noticeably, somewhat surprisingly, paunchy
 ninja until he slips on
his ninja mask, at which point he inexplicably
quick-thins and spin-kicks the villainous other ninja
 that has been shadowing him
 forever in the '80s
 series *The Master*, a show

that is—how do you say?—dismal, a hack job so rank
 that two episodes of it
were Frankenstitched together, seams-be-damned, and treated
 as a feature-length movie
by the *MST3K* crew, which specializes
in flopperoos a space-drudge and his robot puppets
 can pillory, in this case
 by needling, scene after
 scene, Lee's sudden slenderness,

and though most of *The Master* is facepalmingly bad,
 at one point, Grampa Lee snags
the arm of some henchman, who says, "The old man hired you,"
 and Lee responds, "I am not
for hire," and the henchman, who is Lee's as-yet-unknown
nemesis, counters, "We are all for hire in dark times,"
 and I think, *Okay, they got
 off* one *good line.* Or maybe
 not. Maybe I just like it

because my self-styled sense of selves—ethical, moral,
 epistemological,

tragical-comical-historical-pastoral,
 plus all -etic and -istic
adjectival permutations, as well as whether
one likes, on a given day, the singe of cinnamon
 or suffers stoplights nobly—
changes, as we change, nightly,
 a stance useful insofar

as it is useful. A favorite word: useful. A word
 I've heard myself applying
like plastic explosives to friends' cockamamie plans
 or students' proposed courses
for Fall Term: *I'm just not sure*, I murmur ever-so-
wisely, *that would be useful*. Satisfying? You bet.
 Morally good? Meh, maybe.
 But useful? No, prolly not,
 and there deliberation

ends because, above all things, choices must be useful.
 Thus, I'm learning I might be
less a lapsed Christian and more a proto-pragmatist,
 although God knows what that means—
when I google "pragmatist," nothing useful comes up.
Even to think my faith might not be in higher things
 but simply up for hire,
 winnable by whatever
 ultimate concern will pay

the best dividends, turns my Inner Youth Pastor mute,
 but Rain God? Sure, if it rains.
A rabble of half-drunk gods and goddesses engaged
 in constant squabbles, throwing
benders and lightning bolts? Not great, but it would explain
a lot. Water-and-waves-style Zen, a cosmic ocean
 to which I'll one day return?
 Honestly, not my first choice,
 because as Andrew Marvell

notes, "The grave's a fine and private place, / But none, I think,
 do there embrace," of which, first,
ditto in cosmic oceans; and second, that "embrace"
 covers a heckuva lot.
"Grant an idea or belief to be true," William
James writes, "what concrete difference will its being true make
 in anyone's actual

life?" Yeah, what does it matter
that I slightly embellished

Lee Van Cleef's spin-kicking achievements for the worthy
 purpose of comedic punch?
That *The Master*'s best line, according to my buzzkill
 friend, is borrowed? That I use,
embarrassingly but indisputably, a few
too many adverbs? Lee's nemesis also declares,
 "The night is always with us,"
 and I feel it even now,
 hovering on the other

side of the planet. One wit summed up pragmatism
 in four words: "What works is true."
Someone else: "Mere expediency and low cunning."
 As for Tiamat, that's what
I named the skink who used to skitter through my garage,
a rain-slick root vegetable pronged with legs: I meant it
 as a sign of respect for
 both lizard and deity
 and, verily, who's to say

that this single act of defiance or deference—
 whichever—won't be the one
that matters most? The working belief I need granted
 true is clearly redemption
because there's, like, waaaaaaay too much David Kirby in here,
yet who's to say one good line won't undo the bad ones,
 the ones rattled off during
 last year's hurricane-induced
 blackout in an Applebee's

running on a generator, all thanks to the God
 of Generators? And who's
to say the girl with amazing dreads won't take me home
 because my one funny line
was the sole droll line she needed delivered? My whole
life I have been banking on the eyes-closed, held-breath chance
 that at my baptism, when
 the priest sprinkled my forehead,
 one of those drops was holy.

Julian Stannard

Three Poems

Buttocks

In the autumn of 1967 a cloud in the shape of human buttocks
appeared over Krakow
—Nina Fitzpatrick

A pair of buttocks forging along Shirley High Street
without feet, legs, arms, without anything—

Only when Adeline tried to sit down
did she realise something was wrong.

Too late now.

She shouldn't have spent so much time
on Tik Tok. She shouldn't have abandoned
Russian literature.

Cut me some slack, the buttocks said
and made a dash for it.
A magnificently large pair of buttocks
with no little swag.
They were going for Egalité, Fraternité and Liberté.
They wanted to sing La Marseillaise.
They couldn't remember the words.

The buttocks drop into Boots
and buy some Coco Mademoiselle.
They make their way down Shirley High Street
in a vapoury halo of lime and patchouli.

Workmen high in the sky with hard hats
whistle so hard
their teeth fly across the city.

A small but growing number of youths
start following.
What a day!
The pied piper of buttocks
swinging their way down Shirley High Street.

Jouissance!

They pass the Pie Shop. Nice.
And the Pawn shop.
Nothing to pawn. Only denim
made in that faraway country
EL-AL Chutzpah.

The buttocks nip into the Black Sea Supermarket.
Welcome, welcome,
when it comes to goats and/or buttocks
there's no discrimination here.
They pop some Bulgarian goat cheese
into a back pocket.

The buttocks pass the Turkish Barber's
and the barbers say
Come in! Come in!
I have no hair to cut my lovelies
Come in anyway, please . . .
We could do a head massage.
You couldn't, you couldn't.

They sail past the Bingo Hall and the Catholic church
and there's the beginning of a traffic jam
and the hooting
of horns but the buttocks are unconcerned
and move with purpose and panache.
They cross the road
and wave to the held-up cars.
They're waving without hands.

The buttocks make their way
to the local library
which is next to Lidl.
They ordered a book a long time ago.

Where on earth are we?
says one of the men.
Shit happens says another.
The librarians smile,
an unusual occurrence.

Why not borrow some crime fiction,
the un-official biography of Prince Andrew?

Why not borrow fantasy? People love fantasy.
No, the buttocks say, we want something by Gogol.
Who? they say.

Google it!

The book has arrived
and now the buttocks are collecting it.
It had taken the library a long time
to track Gogol down who was happy
not to be tracked down
but they'd tracked him down.
Now the buttocks are going
to take him on a road trip
and they leave the library
with some Bulgarian goat cheese
in one pocket and Gogol in the other.

If one pair of buttocks weren't enough
on the other side of the road
going in the opposite direction
there's another.

These are wearing football shorts.
They were tired of losing matches
and just as Alfie was taking a shower
they said Oh no what's that over there?
Where? *There!* And when
he turned
the buttocks ducked and shimmied,
patted themselves down
with a towel, threw on a pair
of clean shorts and legged it
(without legs of course)
down Cawte Road.

If one were preparing
a spreadsheet of buttocks
these would go in a different column.

As if Aphrodite had called on Polykleitos of Argos
saying, I don't want common-or-garden buttocks.
I want buttocks which sail through
the theatre of Dionysius like a chariot of fire—
I want buttocks which shimmer

in the bathhouse like the sun rising over the hill.
I want buttocks which give Tom of Finland
a run for his money.

These buttocks aren't without followers either:
women, men and a three-legged Golden Retriever.

People are opening their windows
and playing that old game lobbing the nut.

(Any nut will do—)

If they hit the spot the buttocks crack them.
Crack! Crack! *Crack!* left right and centre
as if they were setting off firecrackers
in the back streets of Naples
as if they were at the Festival of San Gennaro
waiting for blood.

The buttocks slip into the Misty Magic Tattoo Parlour.
India says I have been waiting for you
and the buttocks begin their lamentation:
Alfie has tattoos
on his arms and legs and chest and thighs
and we're a tabula rasa.

India wanted to put an arm round their shoulder.
There weren't any shoulders.

It is what it is India said.
They are what they are.

Move over Michelangelo, these are mine.
Shall we do the elephant god on one,
and Lord Shiva on the other?

The buttocks slip back into their shorts
throbbing paradoxically,
They carry on down Shirley High Street.

The buttocks in denim head for the Pig 'N Whistle.
The others are heading for the hinterland.

There's a choice.

Oh no, Oh no
choice
is
despair!

A GASH IN YOUR HEAD

What if
you thought you could tie your laces?
But all this time you were just wrapping
a whole roll of sellotape round your shoe and
hoping for the best?

—Caroline Bird

You walk through the city
with a gash in your head.
The crowds part like the Red Sea.
The blood drips on the pavement.
Someone takes a picture
and puts it on social media.
Oh DADA is back, they say.

Did DADA ever go away?

You walk through the city
with your heart on your sleeve.
Heart doesn't look good
nor does the sleeve.
You need psychosurgery,
several therapy dogs . . .
No one hangs about.
The only dog in town savages your foot.

You walk through the city
with an eviction notice.
In the grand scheme of things
it's not a great deal of money.
You don't have any money.
You rely on the kindness of strangers.

The crowds part like the Red Sea.

The homeless man follows you
up and down the street
assiduously.

You walk through the city
with your shoelace undone.
The whole city stops and trembles.
The city has not one visceral clutch

but two.

Your friendly dealer puts an arm around you
like a brother.
Mate, he says, I'm not your mother.
I have to warn you about that lace.
It's a disgrace. It's out of order: it's undone.
You happen to know your friendly dealer
carries a gun.

The bus driver stops his bus
opens a window and shouts
Oi, your lace is undone!

You try and look grateful.
You look sheepish.
So many people on the case.
They want you to bend over
and rectify the situation
without hesitation

The Kray Twins appear.
Footwear impeccable.

On a good day
Ronnie can put his nose in the air
and pluck out that smell in Ravel.

Don't mind us Sonny Jim.
You want a lump of ice?
You could do yourself an injury
What with that lace of yours.
You need to take care of yourself,
What with that lace of yours.

You don't want to bend over

in front of Ronnie
there on the street
arse
sticking out—

You need to find a low wall,
a bench—
you need a little space
a little privacy.
You don't want to tie your lace
in front of the whole city
watching and waiting and trembling

You walk on.

The country's run by liars and crooks.
Across the planet there are wars going on.
There's famine and starvation.
You guess the city's losing interest in your lace.

About time.

A convent of nuns crosses the road.
They're following Sister Marie
and Sister Marie is following you.

The city was having a breather.

You're in the clutches of nuns.
Sisters of Rectitude
Brides of Christ
Sister Marie blesses you—
she says
You don't want to fall over
and have yourself another gash.

Oh my child.

A novice bends
and ties the lace.
Partake of the sacraments
says Sister Marie
and swirls off into the city.

Now your lace is tied

the crowds part like the Red Sea.
You almost have the city to yourself.
You feel skittish
and embark on a little tap dancing
with a gash in your head.

The blood drips on the pavement.
Someone takes a picture
and puts it on social media.
DADA is back, they say.

Did DADA ever go away?

You don't realise the other lace
is unravelling.

Ronnie puts his nose in the air.

Colonel Crust is wearing jodhpurs.
He's a decorated soldier
with a Rogan Josh on his left shoulder.
He waves his stick at you.

Men with shaved heads and necks
covered in tattoos who are capable
of violence are fretting.

Pope Innocent X appears
with a packet of Marlboro.
His boots are beautiful.
He smells a little of the Tiber.
His English is so-so-so.

I'm much concernèd about your shoe.
La scarpa, la scarpa.
You stoop and kiss his ringed finger.
He doesn't linger.

You imagined he'd performed a miracle
that the lace had tied itself
so although you were blessed
you were nevertheless undone.

The Kray Twins
are getting hot under the collar.

Yves Saint Laurent appears
as does Jimmy Choo.
In Stoke Newington
you lie down in the beautiful arms
of a beautiful Jew.

Escalator City

Last month you'd never heard of it—
Now you're there hook, line and sinker
stepping onto an escalator
which is going up and up and up
the sunlight streaking your face—

and sometimes—what longing—you glimpse a city
(a real city) Berlin, Athens, London, Budapest, Rome.

Weren't you glad when you reached
the gates of Hyderabad?

Now you're rising
and then, as if it were a game
of snakes and ladders,
you're going down ...

A moment of reflection—oh no, not that—*reflection!*

One moment you're up like a Tiramisu.
The next you're going down like a plum pudding.

By the way
it's not the sort of place you can get away from in a hurry.

There was, I think, an entrance—

Welcome.

We Appreciate Slow-Walkers, Non-Talkers
and —please note—Staring Is Forbidden!

No point running up the escalator
because you imagined you saw something
plucked from the world—a white horse say,

a house with a garden and some befuddled shed.
Saying shed makes you feel giddy.

Shed, shed-giddy-giddy-oh!

Some people are sent to Escalator City
as a punishment—I did something wrong.

No one used to lie in bed saying:
Please don't send me to Escalator City.
I'd rather shove a stick in my eye.

You've been sentenced to a month in Escalator City.
Oh weep for me.
You've been sentenced to six months.
Oh weep for me even more
Up and up, in search of redemption.
The city on the hill with moving walkways —

Tiramisu with whips!

Some come to Escalator City for therapy.
The rhythms of ascent (Apotheosis)
and descent (Gehenna) etc etc will nudge
the frontal cortex into the right position
and have an improving effect
on the buttocks —a cosmic re-alignment.
Two months of therapeutic escalators
and you will step into the horizontal world
like an evangelical toaster.

You will be new—like a wedding gift.

A walking miracle.

Sometimes the warmest aromatic winds
greet you on the escalator
and your private parts buzz with satisfaction.
On those occasions the escalators
are full of tantalising opportunities.
The next escalator sends an artic wind
which stops you in your tracks.
Oh Lord Shiva what have I done?
Have I not suffered enough?
I'm afraid not, there's always more to come.

The steps of the escalator
are onto you like the teeth of a shark.

There are more announcements:
Escalators are moving pieces of machinery.
Please hold onto the handrail.
Please do not stare —don't fall asleep.
No kissing, no horse play—no horses.
No inappropriate touching.
Please be aware you are about to step off
the escalator—there will be a jolt
as if you were about to leap off a turret.
No turret to leap off —concentrate.
See it, say it, shag it (shag what?)
Escalator City would seem a shagless kind of place.
Sometimes a pigeon zips through.
Sometimes music.
The least interesting songs of Steely Dan.
Some days everybody looks like Bamber Gascoigne.
Sometimes an advert—Are you feeling tired?

Yes!

There are walkways between the escalators
and designated food stations
where they serve durian fruit
and beef cheek with pearl barley (Paul Bailey?)
and reconstituted cattle burgers,
whose gherkins were consecrated by the pope.

And there are lavatorial breaks which are,
without doubt, the most agreeable thing.
Your buttocks are washed with kumquat spray
and dried to perfection by a Kyoto breeze.
You look forward to your next evacuation.
(Montaigne was fond of his bowels.)
The excrement is sucked into the oubliette
which goes down and down and down
to a state-of-the-art recycling plant
and which then climbs up and up and up
in a Nietzschean loop of everlastingness.

Marc Estrin

Gregor Samsa– Hannah Arendt Letter Exchange

Gregor Samsa, Kafka's man-turned-roach, has been sent in semi-roachness out to New Mexico to assist in the highly secret Project Y, where everyone had a secure code name, and the atom bomb itself was called "The Gadget."

A LETTER EXCHANGE

between

GREGOR SAMSA,

HEALTH MAINTENANCE CONSULTANT, THE MANHATTAN PROJECT,

and

HANNAH ARENDT,

concerning

HER PARTISAN REVIEW ARTICLE (v.11, FALL 1944), "FRANZ KAFKA, A RE-EVALUATION ON THE OCCASION OF THE TWENTIETH ANNIVERSARY OF HIS DEATH"

P.O. Box 1663
Santa Fe, New Mexico
August 30, 1944

Very Honored Doktor Arendt:

You possibly find this funny or rude, but two months ago I buy new copy of *The Trial* and try to set on fire. I fill a buket with paper and kindling paper, make nice fire, perfect for auto-da-fe, and throw book into flames. It fast puts flame out, my room fill with smoke, the fire brigade arrive and I have bad time to explain my actions to firemen.

However, I explain to you. I just red your "re-evaluation" in the Partisan Review and feel—while you make certain points against grain of most opinion—you in the end to join a critics crowd who worship an idol that walks on the world with poisonous steps.

For you, Herr Kafka is important Jewish outsider using his only weapon—thought—against a "falsely created world". You see his characters as "facing society with an attitude of constructive defiance, open aggression", ready for taking a stand against such a world "for the sake of human values". You make M. Kafka a man of the Enlightenment, an emancipation moralitist who writes of his utopian, romantic faith in Reason.

But this is surely not true. The heroes of this writer are not ever fighters. The book is fascist and its characters are terible creations of such terible world. What kind of models are they for a reader? Herr Kafka's characters react to the most terifying events as if they were simply normal. They perform their duties without understanding, in blind obedience. To follow the rules is more important than what the rules are, more important than the moralitat of the rulers. In Herr Kafka's world there is no freedom because there is no real self to be free. There is no real personality, no real love. Human beings turn to apes, dogs, moles, mice—even insects—who struggle in ungeklärte interpretations, full of nothing but not-productive hypotheses. This is a world of no-freedom, and whatever transformation Herr Kafka offers leads only to damnation.

I agree with you that Herr Kafka "sounds the alarm" and describes the world "as it is, and as it should not be." But does it make free to portray the madness of the world? Very much not. Mister Kafka makes a destructive, bleak image of the way things simply ARE. He offers no political or social vision, no encouragement for members of any human community, just a nihilism makeing alienation and dehumanization. His characters are victims of inexplicable forces, helpless in fear and chaos. They are not able to reflect. They can only sit "outside the Law", silent and listen.

Herr Kafka's stories may be of service to intellectuals with their feelings of helplessment and self-loathing, but they just justify the ways of a banale, bureaucratic, not-understandable fascist system. Readers could become Mr. Kafka's victims, unfit for life, tied to death, tangled in his endless confusions and confusions not proposeing any solutions to the problems and will never, in Kleist's beautiful words, help humans „Ein Feld zu bebauen, einen Baum zu pflanzen, und ein Kind zu zeugen." His dis-ezed universe, un-penetrable, abnormal, offers no human dignity to a race in dire need of such. Does everything need question, the whole Gestalt of the West?

You and I certainly share the same goal: to free human spirit from dictator institutions and machine rule. But the totale pessimism of this Prague insurance agent, convinced of the impossibility of all assurance—does that serve human needs? In short, Herr Kafka is bad for the world. I hope you will agree, go against current opinion, and truly "reevaluate" this overrated writer.

Highest regards,

George Samson

۞

365 W. 95th St.
New York 25, N.Y.
20 December 1944

Dear Mr. Samson,

Thank you for your provocative letter. I hope you will have patience with the extended answer I believe such a letter demands.

I must admit I found your auto-da-fe amusing, though not for its slapstick quality. Rather it demonstrates an unfortunately typical misdirection of goodwill: destroying the messenger does not invalidate bad tidings.

We agree, I think, on the message Kafka brings to a misconstructed world: the ancient admonition to "Know Thyself." The truth of our time must be disclosed or uncovered from within its all-pervasive and seductive trappings. It requires a scalpel as sharp as Kafka's to do such deep surgery. Modern man stands amidst the confusion of the time and seeks guidance, and Kafka provides not only guidance, but the intellectual momentum for constructive escape.

Let us look together at two of Kafka's little parables, in some ways contrasting, even contradictory, and in some ways additive. Here is the first:

> "He is a free and secure citizen of the world, for he is fettered to a chain which is long enough to give him the freedom of all earthly space, and yet only so long that nothing can drag him past the frontiers of the world. But simultaneously he is a free and secure citizen of Heaven as well, for he is also fettered by a similarly designed heavenly chain. So that if he heads, say, for the earth, his heavenly collar throttles him, and if he heads for Heaven, his earthly one does the same. And yet all the possibilities are his, and he feels it; more, he actually refuses to account for the deadlock by an error in the original fettering."

Even so is the world, a place where freedom and security is protected by chains which, while not seriously limiting earthly activity, keep one from falling off. But Kafka tells us that earthly freedom—that granted by "the world"—is not enough. For there is a dimension of other-than-earthly activity which also belongs to any citizen of the world: he is bound also to this transcendent realm, and gives up his citizenship at his peril. That is Kafka's first great message: not one of limitation, but one of transcendent connection, a connection which also protects from too great immersion in the ordinary. True, there is conflict, tension, even paralysis in this situation, and you, Mr. Samson, may see the protagonist as defeated by his sadistic author. But the protagonist is not defeated. He is actually aware of the possibility that there is no error in the structure, that if deeply perceived and adroitly handled he may be able to bountifully operate within these strictures, as a poet does within the limitations of sonnet form. It is not stubbornness or stupidity behind his analysis. It is the smell of real freedom.

The second story is this:

> "He has two antagonists: the first presses him from behind, from the origin. The second blocks the road ahead. He gives battle to both. To be sure, the first supports him in his fight with the second, for he wants to push him forward, and in the same way the second supports him in his fight with the first, since he drives him back. But it is only theoretically so. For it is not only the two antagonists who are there, but he himself as well, and who really knows his intentions? His dream, though, is that some time in an unguarded moment—and this would require a night darker than any night has ever yet been—he will jump out of the fighting line and be promoted, on account of his experience in fighting, to the position of umpire over his antagonists in their fight with each other."

The most obvious level of this tale concerns man embattled between the forces of the past and the imperatives of the given future. It pictures a crushing, suffocating thought-world miraculously evaded. However you choose to interpret the story, Mr. Samson, it again urges corrective action. True, the night will have to be at its darkest—to provoke, to inspire and to hide—but such a condition is already a regular occurrence in our dark times. And the man who can dream such a jump, such a discontinuity, such a transformation, that man is more than halfway toward its realization. Let Kafka whisper in your ear, and things may evolve which have never appeared before.

Forgive my presumption in suggesting that you concentrate not on the fetters, or the darkness of the night, but rather on the taut potential for situational metamorphosis. Kafka discloses what our blinded eyes have ceased to see, and such revelation has the power to trigger the springs of action.

As it has not yet appeared in English, and would be difficult in any case to penetrate, I imagine you have not read *Being and Time*, the work of my friend and teacher, Martin Heidegger. It is impossible to summarize this complex work, but let me alert you to its existence, and hope you will spend some time with it when you can. To whet your appetite, let me simply mention that a key node in the work concerns the experience of "Angst", a word with no English equivalent, approximately rendered by "uneasiness" or "malaise", a feeling of non-normality occasionally experienced by reflective and serious people, perhaps you yourself. Common things may seem uncanny, odd or unfamiliar, as if from some other planet. Heidegger argues that Angst is a crucial experience in pushing beyond the "they-world", a blinding, deafening, stultifying continuum of idle talk and stereotyped expectations. One who is transformed by Angst is given the space to escape such a world—by seeing how strangulating it really is. Kafka's heros are characterized by nothing so much as Angst, and are therefore given an opportunity to transcend denied to most people. Inasmuch as the reader identifies with these characters, they too, are asked to see the world as unheimlich—uncanny, but also etymologically "not-at-home", and themselves as no longer unquestioning members of the "they". Kafka's animals are the supreme metaphors of potentially redemptive self-alienation. The animal metamorphoses you mention—into "apes, dogs, moles, mice—even insects" are not simply "regressions"—these characters are adventurers out of the "they-world" into the possibility of other experience and deeper understanding. There may be many "unresolved interpretive furies" and "unproductive hypotheses", but Kafka's writing would not be "true" were it otherwise.

You may be interested in Heidegger's understanding of the fruits of Angst, painful as they may be. Angst draws out, e-ducates, the authentic self, which then interacts with an authenticated world via Sorge, or care, both caring-about and caring-for.

Again at the risk of being presumptuous, let me say that you seem to be a caring person, perhaps just by nature, or perhaps after having experienced some kind of transformative Angst. My counter-suggestion to you is that you be the one to re-evaluate this extraordinary prophet and teacher, and to engage him not as an enemy, but as a friend. "An enemy," as the Russian proverb says, "will give in, but a friend will argue." Kafka never does give in, does he?

I remain yours sincerely,

Hannah Arendt

Andrew McKeown

Pastoral

Moyes came out of the shed holding an air pistol. He leant forward and compressed the sprung barrel against the concrete path, then unscrewed the breech pin and loaded a dart.

'Say hello to Mr Gat.'

The barrel shot forward.

The sparrows were unmoved.

Moyes reached down to the cage, put his hand underneath and recovered the yellow dart from the grass.

This time he said nothing.

On the second release, the cage gave off a sharp, metallic ring, but still the birds went on pecking at the biscuits.

'You have a go.'

Moyes handed the gun to Judd.

With the dart once again extracted from the grass and the barrel reloaded, Judd took aim.

The three birds had formed a single mass.

The barrel shot forward a third time, projecting a dull bolt of sound that came to nothing.

'You missed on purpose.'

Moyes eyed Judd with his characteristic leer, then turned away.

'Fuck this for a game of soldiers. Come on, let's get the fishing stuff.'

Moyes had thick, purple lips and a haggard face. The other kids on the street referred to him as *the boy with a hole in his heart*. He, Judd and his brother had arranged to go fishing that afternoon.

Beyond the new-built streets, the fields were overgrown with long, summer grass. Hedges merged and broke apart across the view. Sometimes, hanging from wire fences, the pelts of voles were to be seen. Ponds—old marl pits or holes dug to provide water for cattle—dotted the still, heat-shimmering land. Only the broadcast of skylarks could be heard, and beneath them Moyes, talking about his last outing:

'The far pit's the best. Loads of rudd and perch. Took one home last week and ate it. Mum fried it for us. We'll head there.'

Looking out across a dual carriageway and, beyond that, another, raw estate of houses, the pond was located at the northern edge of the fields in which the children played. In spring they came bird-nesting in the copse behind the place where the rag and bone man lived. In winter they came to skate across the ponds. As Moyes spoke, Judd recalled the alien echo of the frozen vault that creaked under his weight, the thrill of fractures radiating out from his shoes.

'Plus, it's good for bait.'

They walked on, parting the grass with their bare legs as they went.

The sun was directly above them when they got to the pond. Moyes started setting up his rod, selecting things out of containers and boxes. He handed Judd's brother a net:

'Frogs. Get some frogs.'

At the water's edge the earth had been churned by cows' hooves, forming a muddy clearing. Left and right, pond weed and reeds grew in abundance, and beyond them water lilies, their oriental discs occasionally pierced by white and yellow flowers rising on a stem.

As Judd's brother stepped toward the water, the flat lily leaves to his right undulated suddenly. Plip. Further along more leaves moved. Plop.

'Aim for the rings they leave behind.'

Moyes was holding a penknife, watching Judd's brother:

'Just stick the net in and yank it out sharp. They're frogs, not rabbits.'

Judd's brother attempted two, three passes in the water, across the ripples the diving frogs had made:

'They're too fast.'

Judd looked down. A set of web-footed back legs pushed away into the dark water in the middle of the pond. Then another.

Moyes was growing impatient:

'Try under the reeds.'

Judd's brother inserted the net deeper this time. A coffee-coloured cloud ballooned up to the surface of the water. As he extracted the pole, thick slops dropped from the net he was holding. The smell of disturbed silt was soon in their noses.

'Pah. Let me try.'

Judd took the stick. Going down on his haunches, the boy let the net sink gently at the edge of the deeper water. Moyes crouched down also.

This time they waited.

'Got one.'

Deftly Judd withdrew the pole from the water and was cupping the mesh in his free hand. Inside squatted the bulbous, unlikely quarry.

'Oh no you don't.'

Moyes brought his hand down rudely over the opening, just as the animal sprang up on elastic legs.

'What do you want frogs for anyway?'

Moyes had already taken the small thing into his grasp. Reaching into his tackle box, he drew out a dirty tin, and, pinching the frog between his fingers, set it inside, while, with his other hand, he applied the penknife he had been holding.

At the end of the operation Moyes held out a small section of bloody, olive-coloured body:

'Perfect bait.'

Into this he twisted the hook on the end of the line that he cast into the centre of the pond.

'You'll see.'

I t was an hour or so later. Moyes had left them:

'I need a dump,' he had proudly explained.

The heat of the afternoon was sifting downward toward the horizon, giving a lazy blur to the familiar contours. Judd and his brother had watched Moyes extract several fish from the pond, unhook them with an agile twist of his fingers then cast them negligently into his keeping net.

'Rudd,' he commented each time, a gold-glinting body with orange fins cupped in the palm of his hand. 'Can't eat them.'

The brothers lay on their backs in the warm grass. Judd attempted to place the skylarks he heard calling high overhead, but without success.

'Great day for the race.'

The voice behind them was new, insinuating.

Judd turned and saw an overweight man in a shabby tracksuit with big, swollen eyes. There was a pause. The man was smiling.

'What race?' Judd finally asked.

'The human race.' The stranger offered no response to his own little joke and sat down beside them, dangling his legs over the edge of the bank.

Judd's brother sat up. Judd followed and noticed that the man was rather old and that in spite of his sports clothing he wore town shoes.

'I can see you boys are interested in fishing.'

The man was peering into the keeping net, and spoke with an air of being casually informed:

'These ponds are full of fish in summer. Rudd mainly. Some perch. My favourite's trout. Brown trout.'

Judd looked up from the man's shoes.

'You can catch them bare-handed, you know. No need for rods and lines.'

The man checked the brothers were listening then continued, nodding to where he was sat:

'This bank here. It's an ideal spot. You lie down on your front, nice and comfortable, see, and reach in.'

The man had got on to his hands and knees and was stretching himself out flat on his belly. He looked back at the boys as he crooked his right arm over the edge of the bank.

'Get your hand in among the little roots and tickle with the tips of your fingers. Like this.'

The body of a wide-eyed fish swimming into the fingers of a fat human hand flickered in Judd's mind.

'Cup your hand, ready for him. You'll feel him nosing in, slippery and warm and firm.'

The man was still fixing the boys with his distant yet intent gaze.

'When he's in good and proper squeeze him tight—tight!—and whip him out.'

The stranger jumped clumsily to his feet and turned towards them, holding up an empty, clenched fist.

There was a moment's pause. Judd and his brother exchanged glances.

The man began again, raising his voice slightly as if he were alluding to something everybody knew:

'I bet you boys have already tried it, haven't you?'

He turned first to Judd:

'I bet your brother has. I bet he's shown the girls already.'

So saying he switched to Judd's brother:

'I'm right, aren't I? You've shown all the girls, haven't you?'

Judd's brother felt a momentary inclination to allow himself to boast. He was flattered by the idea he had prowess in something which he had demonstrated to girls. Judd sensed he was being left out and chafed under the impression that there was a skill he was lacking.

'I'll bet you have all the girlfriends, though. Am I not right?'

The man had now switched his attention back to Judd.

'They always go for the quiet ones. I know what they're like.'

Saying this, the man began to speak freely about girls, about the girlfriends he'd had as a boy, how many he'd had and the clothes they wore. There was nothing he liked so much, he said, as the way they had of shaking their hair and letting it tumble all about their shoulders and their arms. Their soft skin. Their sweet eyes. How they might laugh, and laugh.

The man broke off. The succession of words he had been pursuing, like phrases he had memorised, was left suspended in the afternoon air. There was an expression of comical sincerity in his globulous eyes, of a distant pain he wanted to share.

Judd noticed the amused expression his brother was trying to suppress.

Suddenly the man turned again to the boys:

'And you young lads, too. Oh yes, I know you young lads. Out in the fields all day. Getting up to all sorts.'

The man's voice broke off again.

After yet another pause he gathered his breath and, casting his eyes furtively right and left, started to walk away, saying that he had to leave them for a while.

I t was then that Moyes returned:
'Who was that?'

'Some old tosser.'

Judd's brother was laughing:

'Trying to show us how to tickle for trout.'

'Tickling for trout!' Moyes was laughing too. 'There's no trout in ponds. Guy's an idiot.'

Moyes looked back in the direction the stranger had taken:

'Look what he's doing now.'

All three looked toward the end of the field where the man had stopped.

'Told you. Guy's a perv.'

Judd felt he should laugh too, though the full nature of the joke was still not clear to him.

Moyes turned and began to pack away his things. The fish in the keeping net he released, watching them slowly turn back into the water, one of them whipping the sprung coil of its entire body, breaking the pond's surface.

Judd was helping to pack away the tackle and was still considering the sight of the man at the end of the field when Moyes spoke:

'Here he comes again.'

The man was coming toward them slowly, his hands thrust into his pockets.

'Did you have much luck, boys?'

This time he had stopped at a certain distance from them and spoke as if they had never met.

Moyes was the only one to answer:

'There's no trout here. Piss off back to where you came from.'

Judd was afraid the man would think that he was of Moyes's ilk, that he, too, would speak to strangers in such common terms. His face gave him away:

'What's the matter with you?' Moyes had turned on him. 'Guy's a bender. Needs a good kicking, if you ask me.'

Moyes then switched his attention back to the man and raised his hand as if to throw a stone:

'Go on, fuck off.'

The stranger took two or three steps backward and stumbled, then turned and hurried away.

Judd's brother looked across at Moyes and spoke:

'Like that other idiot in the hat round back of the shops: "Do you want me to get you lads some cider?" '

Judd was listening carefully, but was conscious he was outside the circle. Inside it there were Moyes and his brother and the poorly-dressed stranger, too. He was further at a disadvantage for he had always kept a wary distance from Moyes and now it seemed he had done them all a service in chasing away the uninvited man.

'What about the birds in the garden?'

Judd thought he had detected a way out of this debt.

'You what?'

Moyes looked at Judd sourly, then saw another opening and went along with the game:

'They'll be stuck till it goes dark. Then the cats'll come.'

Judd had to wait.

'They'll try and get a paw underneath, but they'll end up flipping the cage over. Fly away Peter, fly away Paul.'

The group walked across the fields back toward the houses, the sultriness of the day settling about their legs as they progressed.

Judd was cornered by Moyes's expertise. There was no demuring. In any event he knew he should keep the occurrences of the afternoon to himself when he got home, though if his mother asked, and here his mind felt refreshed, he could repeat the man's little joke about the human race, and take credit for his sense of humour and how grown up it made him sound.

COLIN GEE

OVER THE HORIZON

There appeared before him where he sat hunched over the body in the clearing a tiny man who cajoled him to put aside his frowny face and look upon the rising of a new day.

What happened to you, sneered the little man, a leprechaun in old-fashioned clothing, stepping right up to him and the corpse he had been dragging through the forest at the end of a rope. Why you crying?

So he explained to the little man that this was his father who had died of old age and sadness and he had no tools with which to fashion him a proper grave for all they would give him in town was this rope to drag the carcass off so it wouldn't stink up the street, the mother fuckers.

I'll be a Christmas ham, swore the little fellow, orange beard wagging up and down with the motion of his tiny jaw, What motherless sons of bitches, and he told the man that he could help the man, if the man could make a promise.

Are you in league with Satan? the man inquired, instantly suspicious of the stranger, wiping his shuddering eyelids on a sleeve and peering at the imp for the first time through his blinking, chewing face. Are you offering to help me in exchange for total control over my eternal soul, or a promise to subjugate my body to the powers of darkness?

Yes, replied the little man, all of the above. But it is not as bad as it sounds, he hurried to add, seeing the man convulsed by repulsion, and a heavy queasiness. The little man said, We have an enormous library.

The man (the son) held himself stiff and quiet when he heard the word LI-BU-RA-RY, feeling in his pocket for his only earthly treasure, a bound volume of poetry by Beatrice.

We even have Beatrice, smiled the gnome in his forest green livery and smock and miniature codpiece, nodding to the man's hand where it worked herkily in the pocket of his coat.

Does your Lord have, have *The Ploughed Cob and Other Stories*? the man asked with a trembling voice, sleeves not even covering his hairy wrists, loincloth loose and crusty and low slung upon his hip.

Does he have *The Ploughed Cob*? barked the small stranger in laughter, removing a small pipe from an inscrutable pocket, sweet Jesus the things you say! My Lord has the *Collected Letters*, not to mention all of Beatrice's other poetry and some of her very rare volumes of prose, said the little man.

And do you have nice upholstered chairs for reading, asked the son, scooting forward on the log where he had been slumped and weeping, and lamps?

We have nice upholstered chairs for reading, replied the imp and jolly fellow, reading lamps, and food from your own countrie.

My own country, said the man hollowly, picturing windmills and unbelievably putrid cheeses.

Thy own countrie, said the imp man.

And you can help me bury my father? the son asked.

And I can help you bury your father, confirmed the urchin, puffing on the pipe now, loving it, thrusting one little leg arrogantly forward in its green tight—looking approvingly at his small, brawny thigh. Spitting on a shoe and shining it with a green hankie, he said, So what do you say?

The man opened his mouth to speak, and that is how I ended up in this dungeon, strung up by the nipples.

What's your story?

SHYA SCANLON

CREATIVE NONFICTION

It reminded him of the time a famously irascible novelist had taken a cheap shot at creative nonfiction by proposing to write an essay delimiting the connections between a) the basketball player John Stockton, b) the spectrum of blue made available by the gloaming in the Yorkshire Dales of North England, and c) Neanderthal grieving. The irascible novelist's number one reply guy had commented that he'd love to read that essay, "in all honesty," to which a well-liked literary critic responded that every time he read a parodic topic for creative nonfiction, he could count down the actual seconds until someone declared said topic to sound legitimately good, and that this might say something about the state of our relationship to the world, or at the very least mark a turning point in the contemporary essay. The reply guy had then responded to the literary critic in a tone somewhere between defensively sarcastic and obsequious—it was hard to read tone on Twitter—saying "everything is creative nonfiction: the sky, this ant, that one blind llama, the sound of traffic, lawnmowers that won't stop," at which point the irascible novelist had deleted her original Tweet.

Spencer finished his muffin while Tracy wandered in and out of the room looking for something. (Yes, their names were Spencer and Tracy.)

He waved, half to acknowledge his wife and half to wave her away. Class was about to begin.

This was back in 2021, on a Monday in late July, halfway through the six-week summer course Mid-Valley Community College's board of trustees just then considering Spencer for a full-time position had strongly encouraged him to teach. The class, on the American essay, was a gen-ed, so at least half of his students were focused elsewhere, typically business or nursing, but this being a summer course his were also students above average, drive-wise. Spencer looked at the lesson plan. He'd be quizzing them on the weekend's reading assignment, "Frank Sinatra Has a Cold," then leading a discussion about whether and under what circumstances a subject might be seen most clearly when indirectly approached. If you were to ask Spencer if he honestly thought that a subject could ever actually be seen most clearly when indirectly approached, he'd privately acknowledge that, well, he wasn't one hundred percent sure, but he'd remind you about the discovery in quantum mechanics that observation itself altered the state of that which was being observed, and that consequently, theoretically, one might be able to apprehend one's subject in a more natural or pure or honest state if it remained kind of peripheral, if that made sense. If you were to further inquire as to whether Spencer had studied quantum mechanics, he'd happily admit that he had not, but suggest that you were being argumentative or condescending or both.

At nine o'clock, Spencer launched the Zoom and watched his students begin logging on. Everything was still virtual then, though there was talk about in-person classes resuming in the fall. It was policy to have your camera on, but not everyone had access to a good or private space in their homes and so the unspoken agreement was to try your best. Mostly, Spencer was watching to see whether Brenda Starling would make an appearance. As one of his students without a good or private space, Brenda was iffy, camera-wise. At least for class. She was not camera shy at all when it came to social media.

Since his father's long-planned murder by the State of Texas back in May, Spencer had been finding it difficult to concentrate. He'd been estranged from his father for over a decade—ever since his trial—and given the circumstances the man's death hadn't plunged Spencer into the kind of despair you read about. His own personal experience of what he supposed technically counted as grief was far less dramatic. It didn't seem to have a center or emotional engine, it just expanded into the room of Spencer's life like an amount of gas too small to poison but strong enough to smell. The therapist he and Tracy went to for couples counseling assured Spencer that grief came in all shapes and sizes and encouraged him to feel his way through it without judgement. This therapist was a Buddhist, big on forgiveness and, running completely counter Freud, believed that identity was determined prior to neurosis, not forged by it. He was fairly woo-woo, in other words—in addition to being a nearly inappropriate hugger—but he was ultimately good at his job. He had a thing of "cutting to the chase" instead of waiting forever for Spencer and Tracy to come to an idea he thought they should have.

Anyway, concentration. He couldn't do it. Movies went unfinished. Books sat open, face-down, draining into his armrest for days. Podcasts were okay, but he didn't listen to them so much as occasionally eavesdrop while looking out the window or scrolling through Twitter. (It looked like Brenda was a no-show that morning, by the way, so Spencer shot his class the quiz and gave them ten minutes.) Somewhere along the way, he decided to give Tik-Tok a try. It was as though the Internet had until then just been warming up, and had in this platform found a way to fulfil its mission and fully flatten the mind. It was a revelation. It was perfect. Spencer became an addict.

Once the class had turned in their quizzes, Spencer asked what they'd thought of the piece. The start of in-class discussion is always a little awkward, as you know, but he'd learned to give them room to be thoughtful. He gazed broadly at the screen's Brady Bunch grid of students, looking for subtle motions that might indicate some internal rumination, a tilt of the chin, a frown at the lip, a skyward eye, but everyone was perfectly still; it wasn't until he jerked into someone's half-finished sentence that he realized his screen had frozen.

"Sorry, Patterson, can you repeat that please?"

Patterson Nati was a young man from Eritrea, often the first person to speak.

"The story makes it seem like Frank Sinatra is a very lonely man."

"Interesting. How do you mean?"

"He has all these people around him, right? But he doesn't seem to be close to them. He's always joking. I feel very bad for a man who surrounds himself with so many people but has no friends."

"I definitely think there's something here about the irony of celebrity. Anyone have any thoughts on Patterson's observation?"

Again the class was silent. Tracy popped her head in the door of Spencer's office and pointed at her face and mouthed something incomprehensible containing the letter L, to which Spencer gave a tiny but hopefully noticeable shrug and mouthed *are you kidding me*.

"I think he seems like an asshole."

Deidre North was still in high school and taking college courses through Running Start.

"Okay, Deidre. That's valid, but could you unpack it a bit?"

She rolled her eyes. Everything was obvious to Deidre.

"He treats people like shit. He throws his weight around for no reason. It's like, leave the boots guy alone! He likes the boots!"

The boots guy was a reference to a scene in which Sinatra picks on a stranger shooting pool for being underdressed, singling out the man's boots for ridicule. (Sinatra is reported to have asked, like a schoolyard bully, "You expecting a storm?") The boots guy turns out to be a young Harlan Ellison, hot off the heels of his first big screenplay and en route to becoming an award-winning author of science fiction with a reputation for being combative—Spencer had always assumed that the interaction with Sinatra and subsequent inclusion in the widely read *Esquire* piece had in fact been partially responsible for not only the reputation, but the man's actual attitude on some subconscious level.

There were some murmurs of assent, but another student spoke up in defense of Sinatra, saying that his behavior was just because he had so much pressure on him at all times to be perfect, at which yet another student scoffed, and look, the fact is that this story isn't about classroom dynamics. It shouldn't surprise you brainiacs that students in an entry level course in a community college are going to have a hard time moving past the judgement phase when considering a piece of nonfiction. Really what we want to do is pan over to where Spencer's mind was wandering while he was half-listening to his class argue about the character of Frank Sinatra.

The TikTok thing spun out of control almost immediately. Spencer would be, say, waiting for his coffee to brew, just standing in the kitchen, morning light, quiet house, cold feet, and start flicking through, and before he knew it his coffee was not only brewed, it was cold, and it was in the midst of this addiction that Tracy suggested he look up his students. Spencer had been complaining about the fact that he'd never met his kids in person, how the lack of physicality stymied the teacher-student relationship because all those casual exchanges in class constituted an entire economy of indicators that could be spent determining the real opportunities and barriers for learning.

"Not sure it's a great idea," she said, "for a teacher to bemoan the lack of physicality."

"My point is I feel like I can't get to know them."

And here she jutted her chin at the phone Spencer was even as they spoke greedily flicking through. "You could stalk them on that stupid app."

So it was settled.

"What can we say about this essay," Spencer said presently, interrupting what had devolved into an argument about proper evening attire, "beyond making value judgements about its subject?"

You might be surprised to learn that Spencer had never really set out to become a teacher. He'd never thought much about his future at all, to be honest; it had always seemed sufficiently distant as to require no immediate preparation until, astonishingly, he'd woken up one day living in it. If anything, he'd had routinely negative experiences with teachers—or people in teaching roles, since to describe what they did as teaching often seemed generous—beginning with but not limited to his own father, who had been an elementary school science teacher as well as the vice principal at the school Spencer had attended until the sixth grade.

This time he decided to fill the silence. "Did anyone notice anything peculiar about this profile? Anything missing?"

More silence.

"Aren't profiles usually based around an interview?"

"He speaks to a lot of people."

"Yes," Spencer agreed. "He speaks to a lot of people, but not the man himself. Frank Sinatra refused to be interviewed for the piece. So. What do we lose? Anything? What do we gain?"

Deidre spoke up. "There's no way Sinatra would have told him the truth anyway."

"Good. He might be an unreliable source for his own story. Anything else?"

When he was a junior in high school, Spencer had taken an elective called Social Ethics taught by a fat man with a kind of cult following. Word was he wouldn't just teach you the subject matter, he'd teach you how to think, so it was a classroom for nerds and wastoids both, a supposed safe haven for kids who for one reason or another didn't fit in. But what Spencer learned there was that adults could be every bit as needy and small as he felt, only meaner. The fat man ridiculed his students, ceaselessly pointing out their flaws, and even in a moment of praise, the feeling was, his intent was not to support the kid in question, rather to denigrate the rest of the class by comparison. He singled out Spencer in particular for his acne (which was in fact a problem) repeatedly suggesting that he was taking steroids. This was an insult with layers, because why would he be taking steroids? Was he trying to put muscle on his flimsy, unathletic frame? Why would he care? It impugned not only his body, but his character, and Spencer had long forgotten everything he learned in that class but could remember the teacher vividly, the way his daily chocolate muffin sat sweating on his desk.

Another case in point was a college professor who took special interest in Spencer. He had several classes with her, all philosophy, and it was with her encouragement that he picked up a double major. He would linger at her desk nominally to gut-check his understanding of some idea not covered in class—that a text had no fixed meaning, say—while privately thrilling at the heady mentorship itself, the kind of classic, maybe a little cliché, student-teacher dynamic he'd always sought but which had until that point proven elusive. But after graduation, he'd found himself at a faculty party where, over a glass of wine and a clandestine cigarette on the back porch, she'd made a pass at him, thus shoehorning their relationship into a different kind of cliché altogether. After he'd demurred, humiliated, his mentor had smiled and apologized, and before heading back

into the house had said, simply, "Couldn't hurt to try." Before leaving, Spencer had watched through the window as she joined a small group at the kitchen counter and laughed, her reentry painless, its meaning fixed. It was the last time he ever saw her.

Those two little vignettes were meant to show you how Spencer's general impression of teaching had been formed. Basically, his feeling was that the teachers in his life always seemed to want something in return, as though education was some kind of exchange. They gave lessons, and in return they expected to be given youth, or at least to get a hall pass for youthful behavior. And this brings us to Brenda Starling.

When Tracy brought her up in therapy, the therapist seemed . . . amused wasn't the right word. Satisfied? Smug?

"Beauty is truth, truth beauty," he said. "That is all ye know on earth, and all ye need to know."

Tracy was nonplussed.

"Keats?" he added.

Smug. It was definitely smug.

Spencer knew the poem. Ode on a Grecian Urn. But he wasn't going to bite. "I'm pretty sure Keats wasn't on TikTok," he said.

"Spence," said Tracy.

The therapist raised his hand. "What do you see when you look at Miss Starling?"

"It's more about what I feel."

"I'd like to see if we can get at what's causing those feelings."

You might be thinking that with all this fuss, we must be talking about pretty racy content where Brenda is concerned. You know, skimpy outfits, suggestive or else flat out sexually explicit, that sort of thing. But it wasn't that. Yes, Brenda was an attractive young woman. Long dark hair. Green eyes. Thin and shapely. Her videos didn't so much foreground those qualities as contextualize them in a culture that had somehow found a way to celebrate the soul-crushing impact of modernity. She was herself, but she was everyone. Almost exclusively devoted to memes, her account was a series of lip syncs and short choreographies, of motions that she had not created but merely reproduced. The effect was a kind of stasis, the memes holding her, perhaps even molding her, as if Brenda was becoming the very pattern she reflected. She would stare out from Spencer's phone, bold and blank, always with the same vague smile that teetered between autonomy and dependence.

"It's interesting," noted the therapist smugly, "that you chose the words autonomy and dependence. When else are we caught between those states?"

Tracy's phone rang.

"Sorry," she said. "I have to take this."

Spencer and the therapist watched Tracy mince out of the room.

The nominal reason they were in therapy was an ultimatum Tracy had given Spencer about his habit of clamming up when in a bad mood, which described much of the previous year but especially since his father's death.

Tracy was ready to have kids, but she did not want to pass along unhealthy patterns and the clamming up thing was one that seemed at least potentially addressable and maybe even solvable in therapy. For his part, Spencer was privately using the therapy to summon the courage to tell Tracy that he didn't want children at all. This would of course be a significant hurdle, relationship-wise, despite the fact that they'd never really agreed on or explicitly planned to have them and it was just something that had slowly become clear to Spencer that Tracy assumed would eventually happen. If not handled delicately, and in the presence of a neutral third party, the disclosure could spell the end of Spencer Tracy—as they affectionally called themselves. Spencer didn't want that, per se, he just didn't want kids. He was one hundred percent fine with their cat Bonaventure, Bonbon for short. Sometimes Bon mot.

The classroom conversation had turned to New Journalism, and how that designation might apply to "Frank Sinatra Has a Cold." Despite the fact that he'd had them read the Wikipedia entry for it along with the Gay Talese, Spencer could sense that his students were confused by the term.

"In other words," he said, "are there passages that feel more like fiction?"

Christina Chu used the hand raising feature.

"Yes Christina."

"'It was music to make love by,'" she read, "'and doubtless much love had been made by it all over America at night in cars, while the batteries burned down, in cottages by the lake, on beaches during balmy summer evenings, in secluded parks and exclusive penthouses and furnished rooms.'"

"Good, good. Why did you pick that passage?"

"Because it's beautiful."

"I agree that it's beautiful, but can't anything be beautiful?"

He didn't blame them for being befuddled. Wasn't everything kind a gray area those days? The personal essay had become increasingly personal. Alternative facts were a thing. The irony was that Gay Talese would have had a hemorrhage if he'd been alive to witness the blurring, the degradation of the boundary between fact and fiction. Spencer thought of what the well-liked literary critic had said on Twitter. Was it that creative nonfiction had indeed jumped the shark after having achieved a zenith of cultural relevance, or had it instead achieved a kind of Fukuyama-esque end state and, like late-stage capitalism, was now able to devour its own critique? (We of course know the answer to this now, but Spencer was seeing this play out in real time.)

"It's speculative," said Patterson.

"Ah ha! Go on."

"The author didn't, you know, see any of that happen. He's just making it up."

"It comes down to that one word, doesn't it. *Doubtless*."

The therapist didn't speak while Tracy was out of the room because this was not Spencer's personal session, it was for the couple. The therapist's office was almost offensively bright. It was a place shadows go to die. Outside the large, south-facing window sat a mostly empty parking lot, and beyond that, a water feature, and beyond that, Route 212, and beyond that, a diner that Covid had run out of business. A couple years before, he and Tracy had stopped there on a lark—it wasn't their kind of place—and they'd laughed at the sad, soggy fries and grilled cheese sandwiches they were served. They'd only picked at the food, but when the waiter had brought out a to-go container with their check, they'd both suddenly felt guilty packed it up.

When Tracy came back in, the therapist glanced quickly at his watch. "Let me cut to the chase," he said. (See? It's kind of refreshing, therapy-wise.) "This interest you've taken in your student's TikTok account is almost certainly a way of processing your father's death."

The sound Spencer made just then wasn't quite a guffaw, though that's how it began. It almost like a bird call. It started somewhere deep in his face and used both his throat and his nose to emerge. It was an ugly, embarrassing sound.

"Sorry," he said.

Shortly after his father had been put to death, his mother had called him. They'd been divorced for over ten years, but they'd spent decades of their lives together, after all, and she was reasonably distraught even given the circumstances. "You know," she'd said, "your father loved you very much. He was very proud of you."

Since his father had always hated teaching, had felt it was beneath him on an almost spiritual level—especially as practiced on an elementary school level—Spencer wasn't sure, at that moment, which was true: that his mother was lying to him, or that his father had lied to her. He was also not sure whether, were it the former, her lie would have been to reassure her son, or to assuage her own feelings of shame. And if his father had lied to her? It could have been either to insulate her from his true feelings, or to insulate himself. Perhaps, for the sake of argument, the lie had actually been built around some small kernel of truth, a fiction that surrounded fact like a callous, built up over years of worrying, of drawing the curtain back to obsessively marvel at its exaggerated smallness, then forth to shield all parties from its tiny flickering flame, blinking in and out of existence, gasping for breath. Spencer could imagine that. It felt generous, but he could imagine it.

Brenda Starling raised her hand.

Spencer hadn't even noticed that she'd joined the class, and since she hadn't turned her camera on she remained a small square framing the initials BS. His pulse quickened.

"Yes, Brenda."

All of this is of course from Spencer's best-selling memoir, *A Teacher's Teacher*, in which he goes on to de-scribe how Tracy ultimately couldn't forgive him for the kid thing, and to frankly defend his subsequent decision to pursue (unsuccessfully) a relationship with his student in order to fully explore the issues he had with his late father, who as you all probably know was put to death for entering his school the day after retirement and killing five colleagues, including the principle, in the faculty lounge. But some information has recently come to light that casts the veracity of Spencer's memoir—at least some aspects of it—into question. Namely, it appears that there may never have been a Brenda Starling.

For those of us who've read and admired the memoir—it won several prizes and was a finalist for the Pulitzer, so, you know, we're not talking about pulp here—this has come as quite a shock, in part because of the palpable nature of the author's depiction. We never did have the TikTok videos themselves, because the account was said to have been deleted at the time of the book's publication, but we had his lovingly rendered, highly detailed descriptions of them. Like the one—I won't do it justice here, I'm afraid, but just to give you an idea—in which she was wearing a fuzzy kind of hairband with little white cat ears and long soft flaps that cascaded down the side of her face and over her bare shoulders and down her chest. She stares directly into the camera (she did this in most of her videos) and uses a filter to give her skin cute little freckles and her eyes a large, watery, glowing effect. She looks curious, alert, head tilting to one side and then the next as she apparently speaks to someone off-camera.

"Rowr," she says.

"Rowr?" responds the voice, male. "What are you?"

"A dinosaur," she says, though her pronunciation is adorably wrong. At this point it becomes clear even to someone who hasn't seen the meme that she's just lip-syncing to some exchange between a parent and child.

"A dina-what?" asks the father.

"A dinosaur?" she asks, again with the adorable pronunciation but now unsure of herself. It's more like *diana-sowar*, maybe, because there's two syllables too many.

But at this point the father understands. "Oh!" he says. "You mean like from Jurassississic Park?"

She nods, again, adorably, not understanding that the father, who is never seen, is making fun of her.

Fin.

You can probably find productions of this meme even today. In fact, the success of *A Teacher's Teacher* caused a handful of memes to enter back into circulation long after their natural cycle had been exhausted. The point is, she was a person (a character, it turns out) who'd left an indelible mark on us, and it will be for each of us alone to come to terms with what that means.

Many consider it a betrayal.

Many, but not all.

Some are pointing to the fact that because the practice of fiction was on the decline during those years, all but collapsing as an enterprise a year later with the open letter, published in the *New York Times* and signed by some two dozen of the world's leading novelists, decrying fiction to be a "dead, irrelevant, even dangerous" artform in which its authors would never again engage, Spencer's insertion of a fictional character—and the way in which that character touched our lives, indeed altered our lives—was a brilliant bit of guerilla warfare, a time-release poison in the belly of the beast, and could in fact herald the imminent return of the novel as a viable medium. I suppose we'll see.

Are there any other questions?

Ah yes, the Keats. Now, in the memoir, Spencer actually comes to an understanding about this, which is that the therapist was suggesting that by embracing beauty he might learn to live with all the tragedy of life, including his father's grisly crime and the way that robbed him of any ability to reconcile with the man. But this depends largely on a straight reading of the poem's final line, which I'm not so sure about. If you read the line as ironic, Keats is actually saying that all the beauty in the world pales in comparison to our messy, painful, inherently finite time on earth. I guess our reading would also depend on how we think the therapist interpreted the poem, but the point is, well, I'll just cut to the chase and admit that I'm in the camp of Spencer got it wrong. But don't let that sway your own personal interpretation! The beauty of creative nonfiction is that we're working with a world of both facts *and* truth. So there's a lot of wiggle room.

So! That seems like a decent enough segue back to the work at hand, right? We've already discussed its suggestion that Neanderthals were far more sophisticated than we normally assume, and that their grieving practices were not unlike our own, which is to say: elaborate and often confounding. We've also talked about how the author demonstrates that although some elements of the practice are universal, others are highly individual. She of course famously compares it to the evening light in Northern Eng-land, and to John Stockton's game-winning three-pointer in Game Six of the 1997 Conference Finals, concluding that grief is destined to remain a mystery forever. Your homework assignment for the weekend is to write about your own personal experiences with grief. The point is not to come to a conclusion, okay? The point is to explore the topic. This is not about finding answers. This is about asking good questions. And for the love of god, please keep it under two pages.

ED HAMILTON

CHICKEN-CAM

Chairman M. T. Husk had convened an emergency meeting of the full board of the Mestha Drone Corp. to discuss the latest crisis that had arisen as regards the company's driverless vehicle line. In attendance were the voting members, captains of industry Dr. Bizaros and Alday Suckerberg, together with various non-entities such as the heads of consumer rights groups, union reps, and the like, invited, basically, to balance out the table and to take the blame if anything went disastrously wrong. Impatient to begin, Husk rose to address the meeting, his baggy suit dropping away as he pushed back his chair at the head of the long conference table.

But Suckerberg beat him to the punch, saying, I'd like to hear the minutes of the last meeting before we proceed to new business.

That can wait, Alday. We have an emergency situation to deal with here.

It's always an emergency, Suckerberg said. He turned to a beautiful, dark-haired woman in her late twenties, blouse open to reveal her ample cleavage, sitting directly to Husk's right and clicking away on a laptop. Hey! Hello there! he called out, stretching across a digital privacy expert to wave in the (apparently oblivious) woman's face. That's your cue, he said. Read the minutes.

She's not the secretary, Alday. Don't annoy her. She doesn't speak English, anyway.

Then who is she?

She's my hair stylist.

Really? She seems to have done a bang up job.

Husk fingered the mussed knot of hair at the top of his head. It looked like he had done it up himself with axle grease. Encrusted with dandruff, gray was showing at the roots. It's Covid, he said. I've, uh . . . well, I haven't been coming in to the office lately, and . . . Okay, you got me, she's a Thai street prostitute. Satisfied now? I brought her in so I'd have something better to look at during the meeting than you two refugees from Roswell. And anyway, at least I have hair.

Bizaros was bald as a cue ball, with bulging, beady little eyeballs to match. And Suckerberg's hair was so close-cropped it looked as if it had been drawn on with a brown magic marker—kind of like what you see on an old G. I. Joe.

I can tell you what happened at the last meeting myself, Husk said. We were reeling, remember, and stock was in free-fall, when one of our self-guided delivery trucks veered from the road to avoid hitting a distinguished looking gentleman in a business suit—choosing, as per its algorithm, the lesser of two evils—and instead plowing through a homeless encampment, killing five, including two women, one pregnant, and a six-year-old girl.

A collective gasp went up around the room. But the gasp had clearly emanated from the non-voting members, who were also supposed to be non-*speaking* members, and so Husk (perhaps interpreting the rules over-strictly) had them removed. He felt justified in this decision, moreover, by the fact that they had apparently not been paying much attention at the last meeting.

After the interruption, Husk resumed: Our initial explanation, you may remember, didn't wash. It was easy enough to cover up the fact that the "businessman" had, in fact, been on his way to rob the bank branch across the street, but for some reason nobody would believe that little girls and pregnant women could be part of a terrorist sleeper cell. As if blood-thirsty psychopathic killers don't reproduce as well!

It's the perfect cover! Suckerberg said. And besides that, women and children can be used as human shields. Any terrorist worth his salt knows that.

Exactly. Which makes it all the more mysterious that the public wouldn't buy it. Current theories posit a sort of "terrorist fatigue" or the more well-known "boy-crying-wolf syndrome".

So remind me, Husk, how'd we finally get out of it? Bizaros asked slyly.

You know very well, Dr. Bizaros, Husk said, so quit pretending. Bizaros had come up with the inspired idea of saying that the truck's algorithm had identified the man in the suit as a scientist who had developed a cure for Covid and was transporting it across the street to the lab at the time of the accident. After all, what are the lives of a few homeless people when measured against the well-being of billions?

Genius! Suckerberg exclaimed.

Thank you, thank you. But the credit goes to our A.I. team, who labored long and hard to work out the kinks. Or maybe to our J.S. Mill Memorial Triage Squad. Although I, personally, coordinated the response, of course.

Of course, Suckerberg acknowledged. Oh, by the way. How's that Covid cure coming along?

People forgot about it by the next news cycle!

The three men had a hearty laugh at the expense of the human race.

Anyway, now's not the time be reveling in past victories, Husk said, refocusing the group. We have a new problem on our hands, and this one's a doozy. Despite our best efforts at concealment in our initial soft launch, it seems the high school kids in Waco, Texas have found out about out driverless semi-trailer trucks. Specifically, they've discovered that these drones will turn off the road rather than run headlong into an oncoming vehicle. Accordingly, the kids have lost their natural fear of the trucks, and they've started to "bully" them, so to speak, forcing the poor gentle giants, rendered defenseless by their algorithm, from the safety of the road. They usually do this along stretches of interstate which abut natural hazards such as gorges or rivers where to leave the road involves the imminent destruction of the 18-wheeler and its expensive cargo. Priscilla, start the video.

Hey, she speaks English! Suckerberg said.

With a few clicks of Priscilla's computer keys, the blinds were drawn automatically, the lights went down, and a screen descended from the ceiling at the front of the room:

The video, shot from the cab of an 18-wheel drone truck, shows an oncoming muscle car—candy apple red with white racing stripes. The car accelerates, bearing directly for the truck. The truck blasts its horn and tries to change lanes, but the car matches it, forcing it right, toward the shoulder. The truck attempts to brake, but it's too late. Instead it veers hard right, crashes through the guard rail, and plunges a thousand feet onto the rocks of the dry river bed below.

Wow! Far Out! Suckerberg exclaimed.

This is better than a moon walk! Bizaros added.

After a few moments, a second video appeared on the screen: same location, same result. Then a third video came on: different location, similar result.

Pause the video, Priscilla, Husk said.

Show more! Suckerberg called out.

At first we thought these fellows were trying to commit suicide. An epidemic of suicide among teenagers. Like in that movie "The Virgin Suicides" with Kirsten Dunst, only this time with boys—so maybe staring Justin Timberlake or somebody like that.

Except that it's never working, Suckerberg pointed out, so they must be complete idiots!

Yes, because they kept doing it. They're still doing it. And then it caught on: they were playing a game of "Chicken" with the trucks. It had become a sort of "Rite of Passage".

Yes, Dr. Bizaros broke in. Precisely. Our industrialized society, divorced from the ancient rhythms of the earth, denies these essential, time-honored coming of age rituals to our youth, and so, instinctively, they find them where they can.

You can't take credit for this one, Bizaros, so don't even try! Husk said.

Besides which, Dr. Bizaros continued, these robots are their new natural enemies. These trucks have taken jobs from their fathers, who sit at home in a drunken stupor watching overpaid athletes chasing a ball around as they dream of the gridiron conquests of their youth. The teens rightly see this as a preview of their own fate. And besides, as football prepares men for war, perhaps these kids sense that we need new games for the inevitable day when machines achieve consciousness and turn their attentions to their fleshly oppressors. In other words, they are playing these games of Chicken as a warm-up for the up-coming tech wars pitting man against machine for the dominance of the planet.

Hey, Justin Timberlake must be, like, fifty years old by now! Suckerberg pointed out.

Let's move on, Husk said. We have a lot of ground to cover this afternoon. Anyway, at this point the kids started posting some very interesting videos. We seized these videos from the kids' social media accounts, covering their traces as best we could. Priscilla, show the next clip:

This time, the video footage shows the drone 18-wheeler approaching from the POV of the car. As before, the truck tries to escape before finally giving in and veering off the road. The camera follows the truck's plunge through the side window of the car, the car slowing down and pulling over and the driver climbing out and walking back to record the fiery wreckage scattered far below.

Then: a cell phone camera is turned on in a whole carload of rowdy kids. They all have beers, and the car is filled with a blue haze of pot smoke. Above the general commotion, a girl's voice is heard: "Joey, I'm scared." "Ah, it's nothing!" a boy says, "These robot trucks are sissies, you'll see!" The camera is turned toward the road as the semi-truck approaches at full speed. The girl screams: "Oh my God, turn, turn!" "Ha ha ha!" the boy laughs, "Chicken!"

Finally: a similar scenario unfolds with the kids all screaming as the truck turns off the road and plummets to its fiery demise. Only this time, unbeknownst to the drunken teens, another car full of drunken teens has been drafting close behind the semi-trailer, and the two cars collide head on, killing everyone in both cars.

Holy Shit! Suckerberg exclaimed.

The Humanity! Bizaros pronounced solemnly.

After a moment of silence, Husk continued: That last one was uploaded directly to the cloud, so no one but ourselves and a small circle of initiates has seen it. In this case we were able to rush to the scene and place the corpse of a recently deceased homeless man, suitably attired in Maga gear, into the smoldering wreckage of the truck.

Textbook, Alday said. But how did you get the cowboy boots on the corpse? I've always found that to be the hardest part.

I honestly don't know, Alday. I wasn't able to attend to it personally. Perhaps they just threw them into the fire after him.

So just a regular truck with some idiot driving. Maybe without shoes. Sounds like a good argument for more drone trucks.

Yes, but this will only work so many times. These are mainly the kids at one high school, Janet Reno High, so it hasn't gone too far yet. Some of these videos have gone viral in China but they have better education, so no need to worry about copy cats there. Our primary object is to stop the contagion from spreading to the surrounding counties in Texas—where, if I'm not mistaken, education has been ruled illegal—either via social media or simple word of mouth. We need to nip this trend in the bud right now.

Hmm, Suckerberg pondered. Bizaros said something about "rites of passage". Maybe we could launch these kids into space.

It's a good thought, but cost prohibitive.

Okay, then, put a gun-waving Magatard in the cab and those kids will back off real quick, Suckerberg said. There's no shortage of them in Texas. And they're all out of work, too because of the robots.

That defeats the purpose of the self-driving concept. And even if it's not a living wage, you have to pay them *something*.

Maybe we could outfit the trucks with makeshift armor and barbed wire and such. Like in "Road Warrior".

Might work for awhile, but I fear they'd eventually see through it. Kids are pretty sophisticated these days. It might even make the game more appealing.

I've got it! the diabolical Dr. Bizaros said. Twenty Magatards is indeed cost-prohibitive. But how about if we have *one* Magatard monitoring *twenty* drone trucks.

But they'll still see that the cab is empty.

Maybe we can use orangutans controlled by a neural interface, Suckerberg suggested.

Still cost prohibitive, Alday, in fact even more so, Husk said.

No, Bizaros said, don't you get it? The truck will engage in aggressive signaling designed to force the conclusion that a *live* Magatard is in control. Upon the receipt of such knowledge, who in their right mind wouldn't back down?

The other two men agreed that the idea seemed promising.

This is Friday, when the teens will be ready to cut loose, Husk said. If you gentlemen are in agreement, I propose we break for dinner and reconvene this evening, when we're sure to catch them up to their tricks. Priscilla, make us a reservation at Nobu for Seven.

Priscilla clicked away on her keyboard. By the way, Mr. Husk, I've quickly researched the issue and, in Texas, sports education and religious pedagogy are both still generally allowed.

Wait, you're not a Thai prostitute at all, are you? Suckerberg said.

No, Priscilla replied, I have a PhD. from Harvard.

Later in the evening, upon their return to the conference room, Priscilla served after dinner drinks as the men settled back into their seats, sufficiently fortified and ready to solve the problem at hand.

Here's the joystick, Alday, Husk said. I'd like you to do the honors. And here's your hat.

But they won't be able to see it anyway, Suckerberg protested briefly. Oh what the hell, give it here. He put on the red-and-white MAGA cap.

It'll put you in the proper frame of mind, Husk said.

Priscilla sat down at her computer and pressed a few buttons. The blinds were drawn on the final embers of the setting sun as the wall screen descended to show a bank of images of open highway shot from the cabs of a dozen drone trucks. The men sipped their drinks and waited. Presently, Priscilla announced that a silver Firebird Trans Am had crossed over the median and was approaching the drone truck on camera five.

Right on schedule, Husk said. Enlarge the image, Priscilla.

Simultaneously, control of the truck was switched to Suckerberg, who began changing lanes erratically, honking his horn maniacally, blowing various sirens, and playing Ted Nugent at full blast over the truck's external loudspeakers. The car did not back off.

They're used to this kind of thing, Alday! Husk said. Act like more of a nut!

What can I do? They've grown up in Trump America!

They're uploading, Priscilla said. I've captured their signal.

Break in on them! Dr. Bizaros commanded. Give me the mic! He snatched it up and said: Attention, rogue Reno High School students, this vehicle is being remotely piloted by a highly competent member of the Make America Great Again Movement! It has been programmed with a Stand Your Ground™ algorithm and will not back down in the face of terroristic socialist threats!

An uproarious commotion from the Firebird all but drowned out his words. They're laughing at me! Bizaros exclaimed, aghast.

Quick, Husk said, tie it to the border wall controversy!

No time, Bizaros acknowledged. You'll have to swerve, Alday!

Shit, okay. Wait, son of a bitch! Are those bastards giving me the finger!? The enraged Suckerberg accelerated. It was too late for the car to turn aside, and so—after a final, chilling close-up of the teens' terrified faces—the two vehicles collided head on. A ball of flame filled the screen as the Firebird exploded, careening from the road and crashing through the guard rail, where the twisted, fiery wreckage plummeted into the gorge below.

The truck, making a slight rattling sound, continued on its way as Priscilla switched it back to autopilot. Each alone with his own thoughts, the men contemplated the screen in silence, the empty highway, viewed through cracked, fused, and slightly charred glass—stretching endlessly into the distance. Finally, Husk signaled to Priscilla to terminate the transmission.

It was, however, Suckerberg who broke the heavy silence: Let's think up a new name for the company.

We've put a lot of marketing dollars into that name, Husk objected.

But it's just the name of an Egyptian god of the dead, right? Dr. Bizaros pointed out. And there's plenty of them. There's Anubis, and Tuamutef, and Kebsenuf. Even Thoth. I could go on and on.

But it's the only one that sounds remotely like Tesla.

Wait, Suckerberg said. No one will believe that the kids are terrorists, right? Crying wolf syndrome or whatever. But maybe we can say they're on opioids. The beauty of that is that they probably are anyway! Then we can just blame the Sacklers.

Hey, they're my friends, Dr. Bizaros said.

Yes, we all love the Sacklers, Husk agreed. And haven't they got enough problems? No need to heap more on them. We're humanitarians, after all. And anyway, don't you think there's been enough suffering today? We have to draw the line somewhere.

In the end it was Dr. Bizaros, as usual, who came up with the best solution: Let's say the trucks are filled with radioactive waste—spent plutonium rods from Three Mile Island in some of them and yellow cake uranium from Niger in others—that would contaminate the entire county if they were allowed to crash.

Dr. Bizaros, what brilliance! You're like Mr. Mxyzptlk or Brainiac 5 or something! (Though you look more like Lex Luthor, Suckerberg remarked parenthetically.) Almost like a god, really.

As are we all, Alday, Bizaros replied with false modesty. As are we all.

And with a trip or two to the salvage yard, Husk added—maybe three—we can easily implement the Road Warrior armor concept while we work on the Orangutan neural interface. Are either of you guys up for a moon walk tomorrow? If we can convince Priscilla to come along, it can be Space XXX!

Devin Jacobsen

Dagonet

"And then Sir Dagonet the king's fool armed him in the shield and jesseraunce belonging to Sir Pigskin, and with his spear and scabbard he rode forth apace. And all the knights did marvel and make merry, and they were passing glad. And when Sir Anthrax soon espied Sir Dagonet riding forth in the guise of Sir Pigskin, he was mickle afeard; and wherefore he set forth his horse, rating Sir Dagonet as he were wood."

—Sir Thomas Malory, *Le Morte D'Arthur*

So this was the end. That's what all the headlines were saying. "The End for Arthur Eugene Dagonet!" For weeks a rumor had hung in the air like a bad stench in the pants of the cosmos, but this morning it had finally come bursting out, all guts, germs, grossness, everything—wet and whistling to the tune of and painting the picture in vivid excretion "The End of Dagonet!"

It had started with a woman. (For is that not how all stories blame their origin? Unless thou believest what came before the woman or the egg must needs be neither, but the fellow coming long ere the woman.) And this damsel, this slutty maiden, being carven to ensnare a good man's eye in the alluring contrapposto of Our Lady of So-Help-Me Tours while sporting the hefty bankbags from a heist of olden days, did lie in wait to catch her a fattened celebrity, and thereby knowing the lad in rut, did pounce upon his fancy. Did pounce upon the unerring truthfulness of his cock. Now it had hit the stands, making the headlines of all the newspapers, blogs, digital babble and chitchat and tweets by pernicious gander, forming the tattle of the talking heads, his own during which—obese, obscene, and oversized smile, the perfect profile of a proper predator—the effigy of a dead god not to be buried but spat upon and chunked to the turds of the East River to drifty far out to sea, where, bobbing, bloated, grotesquely bizarre, it might curl the lips of a passing dolphin in an affect of genuine hilarity and, even more improbably, wash up on the sands among the tribes of Jimbabawe, where he could hope to begin his comeback. Even Jersey was too good for him. "The End of Dagonet!" He was tasting the end all right. Downing marvelous mouthfuls of it (he who was so adept at spewing the shit from his mouth), of antimachismo menstrual murderous mayhem to boot, a siphon for the weeping women and toilet for all manner of clamorous clambaked claims. This was the end of Dagonet.

Thus he was cooking breakfast. Standing boxered and beerbellied and leering down at the slab of French toast (his dick minding its own business, thank you) after his usual morning wake-and-bake and half glass of raw gin and cognac jacuzzi, just trying to get through the damn day without eating two tubs of Alldone's ice cream for the upcoming drama with Meryl Streep for which he was contractually obliged to remain at two-forty and which by now had probably had him liposuctioned from the cast, replacing him with one of his less potent rivals who toted that thirty percent extra schlub and was deemed priapically innocuous, having been rubberstamped by the frigid lips of the Cult of Death. That was what was happening right now this second.

"BREAKFAST HAS BEEN SERVED!" he belted for the umpteenth time—or maybe he had screamed it in his head? It was just so typical. Culture needed a fat little porker for her annual *fête fachée*, and he was the piggy-wiggy who had managed to get stuck. He was paying his dues after living high on the hog, you could say. For a while there'd been signs his career was starting to flag, his ingenuity losing steam; he'd even been toying with the idea of retirement. Maybe he should take this as a sign for a career change? He could be a teller at the Santander (*"Sit on Santander Claus's lap and tell him what you'd like—he's always ready to make a deposit! Ho ho ho!"*) or a monk. Hide away in some select castle by the sea on a remote island, where he could marinate his meat in tranquility and the media would never find him, only the monks. But they would find him, find him funny, ha! *"Let me tell you: It's not at all pleasant for me to be this egotistical and then be criticized for it. I make this look very easy!"*

"IS ANYBODY EVEN LISTENING?" he declaimed, thereupon stuffing the French toast he'd just finished burning, after waterboarding the bread in syrup, in one piece into his piehole.

The articles on the interwebs were saying she had never given him her consent. And yet he thought that when one so lucidly expressed, "May I taketh my dick *en plein air*?" and the answer a "sure, why not," an adult agreement had thereby been bandied in which one succumbed to the shedding of clothes. (Next time he'd call his lawyer and kindly request he administer a syringe of saltpeter directly into his dorsal vein.) Consent. What did that word even mean? A thing that women decide to give only contingent on whether they get to come? He was three inches too short for consent. *It was more an apology than an act of erotic aggression . . . does that make sense? How do you know when a woman gives you her consent? When she smiles at you while showing you the art of a blowjob. No, I'd fuck my own ass if my dick could reach back there, to the asshole. No, seriously, I would do that. I'D . . . DO . . . ME! Already I do me all the time in point of fact. I'm my biggest hoe. We're very sexually active, he and I. We're willing to try new things. Only . . . at the end of the day I wouldn't let him fuck me that way. Because gay-me never gave straight-me his consent for being a faggot.*

He thought: When Jane finds out about this she is going to have a field day, head cunt as she is for the hysterical Cult of Death. I wonder if she'll bring me to court for the terms of custody. Liar: You hope she does.

He patted the procumbent toast, a useless act done with the backside of the spatula, vaguely sexual in origin. Like consent.

I wonder, do we give them our consent? Am I in charge of being willing to enter into this sexual experience? I find that a very unsettling double standard. A very unsettling double standard. Which sounds precisely like what you call it when you're allowed to fuck your wife of ten years twice in a single night. Perhaps he should commit suicide. He'd been flirting with hanging himself only a few weeks earlier. It was supposed to feel quite good, asphyxiating while you came.

The phone rang. It was Dyson. Dagonet tried to complete chewing the last of the toast he was expanding into his waist, but his jaw was tired from masticating, so he was doing his best to savor it. He was as always so thoughtful when it came to his French toast.

"Gene? Hey, all I'm getting is noise."

"Thuuthz chthuzmeeting Frch-thrust."

"Well, I hope you fucking choke on your French toast, my friend, because today is the day we're finally forcefed to swallow our balls, and no amount of Hail Marys or Pater Nosters are going to bring them back."

"I predict this will all blow over."

"You pre—"

"I mean, look, from the outset I've only considered two themes ever worthy of my act: penile feats and compassion. This shouldn't come as a huge surprise to anybody who cares."

"Oh, your coming is a very huge surprise to everybody, Gene," said Dyson in his guilty Catholic schoolboy voice. "You realize there's no pleasant way for me to spin this? You can't put a positive bent on this sort of train-wreck."

"By positive bent you mean—"

"Oh Christ, they're saying others are going to start coming forward now as a result. Do you know who they might be? Maybe there's still time we could buy them off."

"But Dyson," protested Dagonet, slathering a new piece of toast in the batter of his inebriated making before flinging it onto the grillpan like a cumshaw of natural gratuity (he was outwardly quite calm and possessed), "if every time I asked for someone's consent before I was about to give them something I assumed they wanted, I'd just be asking all the time

and never delivering. I'd be no funnier than your proctologist."

"Oh Christ, oh Christ, oh Christ," he was saying, likely at this moment packing his bag and dick up for the long exile ahead.

"You gotta believe—"

"You just don't get it, do you? You're like Rembrandt in the dark. These are very serious allegations of misconduct. This isn't just part of your brand."

"Let me stop you right there, old buddy. See, what does that even mean, 'sexual misconduct'? As if *she's* fit to judge. I may conduct myself like Mother Teresa compared to Buffalo Bill. In fact I misconducted myself last night like I was leading the Trans-Siberian Orchestra with the remnant of a half-eaten turkey leg. Besides, it's like once you've been exposed to one, you've been exposed more or less to all. Kind of like Chinese people. So in a sense she should recognize that everyone's misconducted her. Only why does it have to be public? That's what I honestly don't get. Why does she have to accuse me this way before the entire world? If she wanted the cash, why not just ask? If she wanted to see me in jail, why not press charges or lead me inside a dogcrate? I've helped so many people along the way come up in this business—including, let's not forget, *her*—and they don't realize the mental toll it takes of trying to remain a star, of exposing your soul night after night, and this is the sole thanks I—"

"Let me be crystal clear with you, Gene: No one is thanking you for this. Me especially. Christ, I should have seen the writing on the wall years ago with that puppet-show girl, but then you'd tell me it was only randy graffiti in a bathroom stall. Well, let me be clear with you now, my friend: I am through with keeping your hands clean. This is my resignation. I quit, Gene. I'm sorry, but we—wait . . . if anybody, I'm the one who deserves an apology. I'm completely finished with you, you asshole!"

Thereupon our comic, our tragic comic, our white male upper-class sissily genendered tragicocomicasaurus, levied from his band of *dramatis personae* his most flamboyant Yid, whom he referred to as Mr. Bagel, stoutly against the microphone and matched him fervor for fervor:

"But, Dyson, the comeback tour *is* my apology! You'll see, I'll lay it all out and the goyim will understand! Shylock will have his moneys! I'll even throw in a few spare pounds of flesh. You can pick any area you like, only please spare me my junk. Besides it's unkosher it is, the porker." Modulating to normal. "It'll be a funny sort of *Mein Kampf*. Hello? Dyson, are you with me?"

Dead air. Curtain. He was playing to an empty house.

"HEEELLLLLLLLO?"

"If you were going to be so anal, why did you wake us up so late? I just got out of the bath."

Enter stage left his elder daughter and ex-wife in adolescence, lissom and pre-mascaraed.

"Be nice. There's no need for anyone blowing up at anybody this early in—"

"You're the one who's blowing up! You're blowing up all over the freak-ing internet, not to mention my whole life. I can't even check my Face—"

"Can you please just come sit down and eat breakfast before—"

"I am coming!"

Exit stage left, followed by cloud of abrasive perfume designed to cover periodsmell, in a huff of secret murmurings and whispers.

"But you're not even breathing heavy."

He flipped over the slab of toast after prying its burnt side free with the spatula, trading vestal white for black. *Bite off my left ear, add cannibalizing to yo charges. Sheeet. I got me this pastyass white boy getting fucked up on the backside. They fucking him up real good.* "Jesus Christ," sighed Dagonet to no one, including himself. *What? You think I ain't no real French toast? I's the Frenchest toast they is. Polly-vous franzia, motherfucker? I say Frenchtalk like: Grand Marnier. Chambord. Courvoisier, motherfucker. Been born and raised in the hood up in Cannes. That's why they call me a convict, get it? Sheeet. They frying us up real good. The governor, he eat me alive fore banging the maid.* He didn't think he was probably going to prison; he was merely going to be shunned by all and sundry, a pariah from all acclaim, fame, all major top-tier awards. The only Oscar he'd ever hold would be Mayer. They were taking his adoring fans—a few diehards would assuredly stick with him—but worse, he'd forever be branded a pervert. He'd been a pervert, but now he really was one.

Now no one will watch me. Yes, as in jack off with my penis. What do you think I meant? Practice my tai chi? Fuck you. I've got news for all of you: I got all you guys' consents to be a complete and shameless pervert

when you paid me three hundred green-
backs for galleryfuckingseating, so fuck it;
I'll reach climax right here in front of you,
and I dare you to sue me. I'll fight this to the
Supreme Court. The whole courtroom'll be
covered in unconsensual semen. Mine and
Brett Kavanaugh's. Now where was I . . .

The phone rang. It was Dyson.

"Crisis hotline. Press one to speak to Our Savior. Two to be arsed by Judge Kavanaugh. Three for methampheta—"

"Okay, let me dictate the terms under which I might not maybe be quitting. One: as much as I feel the sting of putting my foot down on this, you agree to cancel your shows for at least the coming month. It could be longer, a lot longer; we'll have to wait and measure the fallout. Oh, and whatever you do stay away from the frigging turncoat media. This Fischer twat who ran the article was practically handed his career on a silver platter when I granted him an interview with Jim Carrey. I phoned him up this morning; I said, 'Don't tell me you don't identify? As one male to another.' And do you know what that prick said? Smug son of a bitch, he goes, 'Sure I identify. What guy wouldn't? It's just that I got mouths to feed, and try explaining that to Gene, that he can't feed them with only his dick out.' Can you believe the balls of that cocksucker? Right, where was I? Point number two: you agree to do a cameo of repentance on, oh, I don't know, say something like *The View*, which would be a godsend, in which case we get the high priestess Barbara Walters to absolve you before God and country for your wayward ways. And three, and most important: you agree

to having this op-ed piece, a rebuttal of sorts and confession, a concession to the hysterical Cult of Death, I had my new intern write published in the *Times*, in which you come clean to having been molested as an altar boy—we won't name names, but seeing as you're from Boston, anyone's guess as to the antecedent is as good as legitimate—and you admit to undergoing therapy for years to curb your problem."

"My problem? *Mais mon problème, c'est quoi?*"

"That you are sexually attracted to women and fail not to act upon it after not receiving consent."

"But I did receive it, Dyson! That's the whole thing! I said, 'Do you awfully mind if I forthwith refresh my dick with some gusto,' to which the gentlelady then responded—"

"Don't say that! For the love of God, please don't fucking say that. Just roll over and admit to everything. I don't care; even if you actually didn't do it, which I'm pretty certain you probably did, admit to everything this bitch is saying and play up the card you've been molested. That's the only way out of this. Just think of poor Paul Reubens. There: I just sent you the file."

"Muhct muh juhstk Fchtuht uh-muhmff."

"You're telling me you can't read with French toast in your fat fucking belchend?"

There was batter and butter all over his fingers. Most pornstars after a gangbang were cleaner.

"Hey, tell your intern I said thanks for having me molested again, but I really sincerely believe once this whole thing blows over a comeback tour will—"

"Why you egotistical exhibitionist! There is no comeback tour if your head is stuck on a pike and they parade it up Fifth Avenue for these raging tribeds—I'm sorry, forgive me, for these people experiencing periods—and there will sure as shit be no comeback if you don't have a manager to sweep things under the rug. Now you will agree to having this published—that or you can kiss your famous fat ass goodbye."

"Yeah, sorry," said Dagonet, eager to get off the phone. His younger daughter of five, Erica, had just sashayed in, still wearing pajamas. "Hey, I've got to go, old buddy. I've got my nuts to scratch." And hung up the phone.

"Daddy, is there breakfast?"

"There is breakfast, peanut. Why aren't you getting ready for school?"

At which moment he realized he'd been eating all the French toast. In waiting for his progeny to manifest, he'd gone on eating. The child was scratching her genitals.

"Don't do that, kitten."

The revelation of the refrigerator's bowels told him there were no more eggs with which to render the batter by which to contrive French toast.

"Why?"

"Because it's not polite. Sit at the table." She bounded toward her chair.

Ever since he'd been a teenager the real meaning of his existence had been a trial of one misadventure after the next, as if the world had been created and designed specifically for the purpose of giving him every opportu-

nity for failure. Of course with women and getting laid, but even with his family and his own dog he had never made solid contact. The rest of them seemed to be going through life rather painless, and their watching him have to suffer, he could sense, made them uncomfortable. It wasn't until later, until college, that he started to count it a gain to be scrutinized from without by people who utterly hated him and who propelled his failures: with in he could at least keep them coming back. And yet somewhere in there things had gotten quite muddled, all turned around. Perhaps the whole ordeal was a blessing, the universe's way of nudging him to spend more time at home with his family. He would buy them a house in the Catskills, where they'd learn the names of constellations and build a fire, say, by rubbing two sticks together. Like gay guys getting it on.

"Here, have some cereal."

"I WANT FRENCH TOAST!"

"It's just like French toast, sweetheart. It's sugary and moist and nutritionally defective. Why aren't you sitting?"

"Because . . . it feels weird."

She was standing, tugging at the crotch of her pants.

"Did you do something to your tutu?"

Her failure to affirm him was an affirmation in itself.

"Rats, not another marble!"

Thus, after washing his hands of batter, after extracting the marble from the dwarf female's hymen as he ran through the multiplication tables (his dick, at times, requested that he be permitted to lend his two cents, but the master directed he be kept at bay), after washing his befouled hands once more and restraining himself from asking, "Was it good?" then after another two shots of Rémy thrown back in the bedroom, they were sitting around the table.

"FIVE-MINUTE WARNING! I REALLY MEAN IT THIS TIME!"

The reindeer jingle of anarchy pants juxtaposed with the heavy-soled pedal point of Doc Martens presaged his elder daughter or vampire version sucked dry by various childhood traumas of his fashioning and neglect.

"I thought we're having French toast?" said the chinadoll. She looked strangely younger, this ghost of Christmases past three sheets to the wind.

"Plans have changed. We're having cereal."

"I don't want cereal," said that black slash mouth. To cover the mottling of the scars she was wearing an assembly of studded leather bracelets, light BDSM gear. Well suited, conceived as she was in whips and chains.

"You have leave to choose not to eat cereal."

"Then why were you making French toast?"

She had him by the scrotum, just like her mother.

"Turns out the bread was moldy."

"Liar, you ate it all. I'm going back to my room. Call me when we're really leaving. Try not rape anybody in the meantime."

"We're leaving right now!" proclaimed Dagonet. "And I did not, DID NOT RAPE ANYBODY!"

As he resumed slurping sugary milk from a plastic spoon, somewhere in that storm-surged sewer of a conscience he wondered what had ever spurred him to be so presumptuous as to think he could improve on his parents' doing. As if simply because he were he he could do much better. Family: a cesspool you take turns filling until all of you drown or expire in the act.

"What's rape?" inquired the child, goateed with the lactate of cows.

"It's nothing, princess," said Dagonet, watching himself speak. He felt the phone ringing. It was Jane. "Shit."

"Is rape an ape?"

He motioned her to hush like you'd fan out a naughty fire.

"You Jane, me Tarzan!"

"Jesus Christ, I can't believe this is happening," said the voice. "I assumed divorce would solve eighty-three percent of our problems, but I literally cannot get away from you everywhere I turn. Tell me it isn't true. It's all over the news. Did you really do what she claims?"

"Probably," said Dagonet, too lamely.

"Jesus Christ, the children."

"Rape is an ape is a grape is a tape is a lape . . ."

Motioning, shooing her. Then getting up and sprinting for the solitude of the shitter.

"What's she saying?"

"I have no idea," said Dagonet. While he ran, ensuring the screening of his junk. "However, I'm beginning to wonder whether you may have dropped her on something unbendy."

He shut the door, locked it. Immediately the cramped sterile space smelling sweetly of feminine hygiene ensconced him in something akin to relief. Then as a deflective balestra: "We had another marble-incident this morning."

Sigh: storm surge of the weeping woman.

"What did you guys do?"

"What did we do? Oh, well, we played ten rounds of Chinese checkers with our lingam and dingum, followed by a long discussion on the anagogical benefits of *My Little Pony*. What do you think we did? Daddy rolled up his sleeves and dove for a pearl in his little girl's oyster. It was traumatic mostly for one of us. I'm gonna need a serious shrink with superpsychic abilities to prescribe me the waters of Lethe."

"Dr. Coffin said she learned it from some boy in school, but I'm beginning to wonder if it isn't an indication of something else. Something much worse. Do you think it could be one of the teachers? They say there should always be two of them there in the room, but the janitors, you know, they get to come and go at large out of the bathrooms however they please. Has she mentioned anything to you along those lines?"

"It's probably, you know, kids just being kids. Totally normal stuff."

"Ugh," her voice was sitting up in her bosom. "Ugh" was the motto of the terrible Cult of Death with two beavers rampant, which one faithfully translated as "All Men Must Die." "You of all people have no basis to judge normality, Gene, not for children, nor for adults. Every year you get ten times worse. Fatter and more a sloven, digging deeper into your most outrageous instincts. And now this. Our marriage was always a mockery, but this simply confirms it. I knew back then you were doing things behind my back, and one day it will be unavoidable for them to know too, for them to see what kind of monster you enjoy touting, but this goes beyond anything like the dictates of art. This stigma, they'll have to live with it their whole lives."

He looked out the window, onto 10th and 23rd. Already tourists were crowding the High Line. Far below a homeless man was leaning against the door of, pissing on the boarded-up Half King. If he craned his too solid neck, in the distance he could barely make out a sliver of the Hudson flowing to the Atlantic, to some other country.

"Look, I . . . I didn't mean . . . I guess I always thought the money and fame would shield them from all the craziness, but now I'm realizing it only exposed them to more . . . and by 'them' I mean the goth dyke and the slut with the very improper marble trick."

Consent. Let me tell all you fellows: there's only one night you ever truly receive her consent, and that's the night you pop the question. That's the only night where you can do anything on the planet, no questions asked. But for a man it's totally wasted. It's like eating a big piece of birthday cake while you're on your way to the electric chair. Who wants a delicious helping of birthday cake when you're thirty seconds from dead?

"So I'm calling the lawyer, and I'll be asking her about going to court. I think sharing custody is a horrible mistake. They should know your environment is toxic. They'll know that already, I'm afraid."

Last time he was in court he signed a DVD, hoping it would ingratiate him to the judge, whom he twice made chuckle in his defense, the whole ordeal leaving him feeling prostitutey and smutty.

"Just answer one question: How can a forty-six-year-old man still know nothing whatsoever about life? What is your big secret?"

The bathtub was still full of bathwater. Alexandra had forgotten to unstopper the drain. On the window ledge lay the hair dryer. Dagonet plugged it in, the appliance a child's spacegun. He entered the tub, underclothes and everything, holding onto the phone, the wet water smelling soapy, barely lukewarm, feeling like some place he was supposed to be, and lowered himself down to the chin, head afloat and rubenesque paunch.

Dear world, I apologize. My go-to hangup: How can I be so selfish while being so damn selfless?

"That I know life's secret," said Dagonet in his voice of honest sincerity.

"What's that, Gene?"

"The secret to life is it's a dirty little secret."

At quarter to eleven the first exiters, a well-dressed couple swinging hands, came out, buoyant and laughing, as they raced to grab the first cab. Within the minute others had followed, and then the rest of the cabs that had been lingering by the Beacon were gone and then it was a race as to who could be farthest up Broadway to hail a cab before everyone else.

They were still coming out and thronging the curb like they were waiting for a parade when Lance came up to the table.

"You've been here this whole time?" He took off his jacket, hung it over the chair, sat, and rolled up his sleeves.

"How was it?" said Margaret.

The waiter came over and took his drink order.

"Okay," he said, extending himself once the waiter had gone.

"Was there a full house?"

"The house was pretty full," said Lance after some thought, "but the applause wasn't as strong as you'd think."

She stopped what she was doing and closed the computer and swept the machine aside. She looked at the man to scrutinize him. How she regarded him implied she held the power to determine whether or not he was lying. Apart from a vase with a single red rose and the menu erect behind it, the only items on the table were her laptop and a cup of coffee.

"Did he mention me at all? Did he say what a shameless, selfish prick he is?"

"To the latter matter: yes. At least a dozen times. Likely several. But so far as the former question: not really. The cueball said nothing whatsoever about the incident."

She spat, a quick blast of air, not quite a sigh, not quite a laugh. What else to say but had you heard the sound from some dentist's apparatus it would make perfect sense?

"That's all you're going to say?"

The waiter came over and put the gin martini down on a napkin.

"What else do you want me to say?"

"How about, for one thing, was he funny?"

The man sipped his martini. He liked playing the game with himself of guessing the type of gin they used in restaurants. Tanqueray, he guessed. Nothing swanky. He picked up the menu, skimmed it. It said the house gin was Beefeater.

"Was he funny?" the man at last repeated. "I'd be lying if I said nobody laughed. But, you know, they were probably his cult of diehard fans, come to send him off with their good will. The turnout of the next shows, you know, once he starts heading south, away from his base, will likely be pretty dismal. Plenty of boos from plenty of protesters."

"But tonight: Was he funny?"

He watched her surveying his expression. Things wanting to burgeon from his brain, wrong little seeds waiting to flower to thought.

"Isn't that his job?"

"Did you ever laugh?"

"Did I ever laugh?" The question itself made him chuckle. The man was her twin brother.

With both hands he held and sipped the martini. If they were still here when he finished the glass, he'd ask the waiter about ordering another with Tanqueray, just to be clear of the difference.

"Once," said Lance. "Just once. Laughed as in out loud."

"And what exactly did you find so funny?" She was watching him the way she had whenever he had stolen into her room and done something he was not supposed to and had no way of answering or defending himself, only to have gone back in time and not done it, she who had been more of a mother to him than his own, lady and lord alike. He scanned the martini, as if in looking he might imbibe.

"The closest he got to mentioning the whole incident . . . well, let me go backward. When he came out he said he was no longer to be referred to anymore as 'Dagonet,' but from now on his new name was 'Tummytuck.'"

"Tummytuck?"

"Yeah, Tummytuck."

"As in he had one?"

"I don't know. Maybe. Yeah maybe, probably, sure. He did look pretty fit now that I come to think of it. For once he was wearing a suit, and he was even pretty cleanshaven. But let's see, the only time I ever recall really laughing—and laughing as in hysterical—was when he pulled down his pants—"

"He pulled down his pants?"

"—was when he pulled down his pants before the audience and showed us he no longer had any . . . any . . . ding-a-ling." The man's lips were folded over his teeth, his eyes small. "He . . . he said, 'You can tell who's no longer *dictating* things.' He . . ." He could no longer talk, just bite the inside of his cheek.

"Are you saying he had himself castrated?"

Subsequent to clearing his throat, "I really don't honestly know," said

Lance with an oversized frown, "but whatever he did, it was pretty hysterical."

Margaret removed her eyes from the man and rubbed her hands.

"Sure, okay. I'll show you something."

She took her computer, which she had brushed off to the side, unfolded it, and instantly the light from the screen illuminated her gaze. Within it there stirred a vitality that was claiming the eagerness of her face into something of a smile. Her brother snorted, reached for a sip of his drink. This calmed him down.

"You've been working on jokes of your own, have you?"

"No," she batted this away. "Read." Turning to him the light of the computer.

"I can't. You read it. I can't see good in the dark."

"I spent the last half hour crafting this to the op-ed editor of the *Times*. It's only a taste of what's still to come. Tell me what do you think: *Dear Editor, With the commencement of Gene Dagonet's 'A Wang Is a Wong Is a Dong: Unrepentant World Mystery Tour,' the writing is clear on the wall. Does the title alone not signify his intent is purely profane? How can a body of discerning critics and audiences not only grant him their easy forgiveness, and for acts for which he has so stolidly refused to claim ownership, but even more confoundingly, offer money at his cloven feet? As has been intimated these last months, there are several others of us who have experienced violations and transgressions—repeated acts of serious harm—at the instigation of this predator, many of whom will soon be coming forward with stories far worse than my own. In the meantime let it suffice those comedy-loving members of the public who have any self-respect and purport a reasonable love for the art to understand that indifference is the purest form of retaliation to Mr. Dagonet's upcoming tour and that they should rally their efforts to prevent making his comeback a victory. Signed, Margaret King.* So: what do you think?"

The brother, tilting the glass of the martini and waiting for the gin to invade his lips, realized there was nothing more left to drink.

"That's good. It ought to hit him right where it hurts. Once they come forward, do you think then you'll end—"

"End?" she cut the man off. What prompted her laughter was glee. "Why this is only the beginning!"

PALAZZO RODRIGUEZ

SIMON IN HIS SPECIFICS

The chair ate everything. It ate pens and paper and airplanes made from the two by the man in fits of winter boredom. It ate tobacco and food crumbs and tight wads of tissue crumpled in his hands during durations of frustration and sniffling. It ate everything. The dog hair and the dander and the dust from books set too long on shelves. It ate the godforsaken sunlight with its deep blue textile tone that bordered on black. The man would like to give it a black and blue, come to think of it. Which he does quite often. Think of it, that is. Maybe he punched it too, sometimes. He'd sit down with full pockets and stand up emptied, an Italian alleyway thief residing in the folds between the arms and seat cushion. These little imaginary games he'd play to keep from grabbing the nearest knife and slicing the seat to slowly descending streamers and shreds. Figured he'd find in its slaughtered insides of springs and decaying support everything he had *ever* lost. Including his health and his job and his marriage. Tried to trace the animosity back in time to when it started. But the chair must have eaten their lineage together too.

Had it always eaten everything? Had there ever been a time where the chair had simply sat, and waited for a further sitting? Was it when he had developed all those gastrointestinal problems after the divorce? That must be it. The chair was pissed off about his ever-inflating ass and the flatulence that came with it. The nights of super processed foods sent out the back end and into the abyss of the chair, to be lost and swallowed with everything else. Must be unpleasant, he might think. Though at this point the struggle between the two had been going on for so long he felt a sort of indignation at having to feel sorry at all. Didn't really. The chair should understand his hurt, understand and accept its Platonic purpose and form, take the farts with the feather dustings and call it a life well lived. But no, the chair had chosen the route of revenge, served stolen. Had taken *everything* from the man. His job, his wife, his purpose. But also bottles of correctional fluid and beer, cadres of dropped peanuts and spit seeds that missed by a mile the ashtray on the side table. And what about all that ash anyway? The dropped ends of cigarettes smoked too long, the accumulating burn holes, the

pain he had imparted on the perhaps once quite pretty flesh of this piece of fiendish furniture that taunted him in its endless patience. The way it waited for the next drop of ember phosphorescent in its falling. Would take all the pain just to be able to also take his favorite pen and hold it forever, leaking ink amongst its tightly wound bowels. Maybe the ink soothed its metallic heartburn, he'd think, some machinic equivalent of all those chalky tablets he popped on his way to or from anywhere, all the time now.

Wanted to slit its stomach open. Crawl inside and live among its guts like a survivalist left adrift in sudden snowstorm. Wanted to sew himself in and bake a pie when he got there. Of all the dropped crumbs and accumulated fluids from French fries to French wine to fake vegetables and needles of evergreen yard pine. Wanted to taste the sedimented years of lost food that could have served to nurture him but had instead been taken by the chair. He'd think he dropped something in his lap, but it was already crushed within the cushion, sent seething beneath stripes that might have once not been so tattered and ready to burst where the sewing had been done.

Felt sorry for the chair, maybe.

But then the anger would come right back. The next time he lost a lighter or a liquor bottle or a limerick from childhood he'd attempt to cheer himself with when the winter slate outside got too cold for even his eyesight and he had to bring some light back, opens his mouth to recite the rote words and finds they won't come. Can't conjure the comedy that once meant he was young. Eaten by the fucking chair. The son-of-a-bitching, thieving fucking chair with its swirls of spit sent in liters from the man's mouth when he'd laugh at a memory he *could* recall. Less and less of those now, because this chair had chosen to take its revenge for his farting.

He'd kick at its stumpy wooden legs and light a cigarette and lug it towards the door as if he meant to leave it at the corner finally, once and for good for all the world to see that he meant business. Wasn't going to put up with this anymore. Not from a chair. Not from a thieving dago of a chair that plotted against him at night and took his things when he wasn't looking and left him wondering about himself and his place and the way he's supposed to live now after everything that's happened has lent an air of despair and desperation to each successive thought to the point he wants to scream, run to the kitchen, grab the knife and yes *yes* take it to the chair in strong swings of stabbing that would leave it screaming even in its inanimate nature which the man, of course, knew was all a show, a charade to show the world what they'd like to see while continuing to taunt him from its tolerant space of patience in the center of the room. Waiting. Waiting to eat his next thought, word, action. Waiting to eat his pennies and straw wrappers and picked debris from his nostrils. The throw pillows his wife had never returned for. The paychecks he assumed safe in his pocket. The sunlight. The chair ate the godforsaken sunlight that he swore he needed so bad this time of year. Eleven days now without it, he'd been counting. Making little Xs on a calendar hanging on the wall in the kitchen. Walks by the stove. Thinks of burning the chair. Chopping it up into kindling and loading it piece by

piece into the oven and burning it all down to ash. But not until he had sifted through the devoured pieces of his life he knew it held inside. Not until he could feel that the chair was sorry for what it had done to him in eating his favorite pen, in stealing all his sketches of nude women he dreamt up in his head, the buttons from work shirts just spent tokens sent skittering down the machines throat, to burble and bubble in the stomach of the chair, wherever it does all its burbling and bubbling amid that maze of springs and false support and cheap stuffing that just kept wearing down to the thinness of a veil with each passing year beneath his ass and its acidic flatulence.

Worried he had colon cancer sometimes.

But sometimes the chair might eat his worries too. It was on days like that he could sustain, for longer than a few minutes, an appreciation for the chair's insatiable appetites. Would stroke its armrest, say thank you, share his cigarette with the seat, hug it and say goodbye when he had to leave for the grocery store, grab a few things, you know, the staples, he laughs with the register kid, setting his pack of smokes, bag of jerky, a can of soup or two on the counter. Looks like another cold one tomorrow, the kid might say as he's walking back towards the blast of frozen air rushing in through the automatic doors, and the man might most likely not respond, and head back down the street towards his home, his chair, and hope it was still in the mood to eat his worries and woes rather than steal a soup spoon.

CLOUDS HIDE LOST AIRLINE LUGGAGE.

EXACTING CLAM

Nick Sweeney

Comedy in Everything

an excerpt from the work-in-progress
Daedalus

"I know London," Stephen told Chaplin, when asked. One never knew what was behind the calculating Cockney's questions—well, Stephen didn't. Nor did Stan.

Euston Station Stephen knew, anyroad, alighting there bleary-eyed from the early Holyhead train and through its grand arch. He paused a while to look back at it and to reflect that it was a *train* station, for the love of Mike, not Luxor or Rome. And the buses and trams confusing when you had another train to catch, and a boat, and a new life to go on to, even one doomed to be fleeting and stuttering and eventually banjaxed. Looking at London, Stephen could quite imagine a gauche young man and even a future genius such as himself going up and down the same tramlines for the rest of his life, mistaking them for the true way but knowing only the ding-ding and dirty looks of his fellow-voyagers. A cab was out of the question for a penniless Bohemian poet *en route* to his Parisian medical studies and his draughty attic and destiny to be sad among the strangers. Station to station, Kether to Malkuth, a brisk gait, a glance at the map channelling him down straight roads: Euston to the river, almost, glimpsed glittering, then the Strand, glorious with churches and stately hotels and shops so full of themselves you averted your eyes in case they charged you to look. Then Trafalgar Square, laid out in its mixture of tub-thumping glory and Italianate grandeur with a triumphal arch—now *that* was an arch that thumbed its builders' noses at you—and a Nelson-topped column bigger than the one in his home town, as was only right and proper and . . . *thoroughly* deserved. The new king up the pink road in the dusty scent left behind by the ould queen—*leave him be*, Stephen thought, *on his silk-covered sack of misrule*. With the monarch one way, he had to take the road that led him to the government, the beating bleating heart of the brazen Empire, with its statuesque pomp, its outhouses, so to speak, uniformed policemen and toy soldiers on toy horses, and Scotland Yard, too, with the police in bowler-hatted mufti—spot the hapless yahoos a mile off . . . and their horses too, no doubt, disguised as oversized sheep, then the gothic grotesque of its lair: urban vernacular, was that? And more churches, begob, the Abbey chock-a with the living dead of the age and the glorious dead of ages gone or merely imagined, and the Byzantine cathedral, unfinished, so they said, that would welcome even a lapsed acolyte such as Stephen if he could name just one Byzantine emperor who bore his own name . . . . He did not dawdle, took it all into the back of his mind till his walk and his map got him to Victoria, the station bearing the name of the ould one and a whole era: an achievement of a place, but a burden, too.

He told Chaplin, "O, I know London. I didn't care for it much."

"Nor did I," said Chaplin. "Ha—look at Stan."

Both men did. Oblivious. Bent over his pad, writing. Content, Stephen thought—no, more, a *vision* of contentment. Chaplin was about to disturb Stan's attention, Stephen saw, so stopped him, a finger to his lips.

"Brings his home with him everywhere," Chaplin declared, loud enough for Stan to hear, the little slíbhín. Stephen saw the envy in him, then. "Like a snail."

"Well." Stephen almost liked the analogy. He laughed, despite himself. "As long as he doesn't leave a trail behind him."

Chaplin stopped his next word, mouth open. Affronted? Stephen didn't know. Not quite, perhaps. Chaplin's look said he wished he'd thought up that one; *I'm the funny man around here*. Then he gave in, it seemed, made an impressed face using eyebrows alone, pointed a finger at Stephen: *you little* card, *you*. He continued, "Not me. I'll . . . never go back." He tapped a temple. "Not even up here."

"Would they want you back?" Stephen wondered—a serious question couched in comic derision. In case Chaplin took the hump, Stephen explained quickly that he wasn't sure you should ever go back if you'd set out to make your fortune. If you hadn't, they felt for you but were pleased, deep down in themselves and yet not deep enough for them to hide it. If you had, they were not pleased at all, and their efforts to pretend to be fell very flat very quickly.

"They would hate it," Chaplin confirmed. "But is there any comedy in it?"

He was baffling to Stephen—and to Stan, Stephen suspected. On the stage, sure he was funny—so was Stan—and only the biggest miseryguts could deny that. Up close, away from the lights, there was no spark of humour in the man, and none of humanity. Stephen was prepared to allow that his mind was working overtime there. Stan came off stage, bereft of the props and the mannerisms, and he was still Stan, but still funny, a mad kind of light deep in his squinty little eyes that would never go out. Chaplin, though? That hat fixed to his head and guarding his cortex, the cane glued to his hand, the man sewn into his baggy trousers and escaping offwhite shirt, that moustache tattooed on him, and those eyes knowing but sad forever.

"There's comedy in everything, sure," Stephen said. *Even deep inside you*, he allowed. *But who will ever dig that deep?* "Even in tragedy." He thought of Hamlet, and the mad theory he had made up on some spot and touted and allowed free to become a legend whose details he had long forgotten. There were gobshites in Dublin boozers now who could remember and repeat several nights' versions better than he, and there was the comedy in the tragedy. "You just need to find it at the right moment. And if anybody can do that . . . "

Stan can, Stephen thought.

"*You* can," he told Chaplin. He sort of meant it. He sort of hoped it was true, but it didn't matter; his listener *knew* the truth of it, and thought about it no more.

Don't rock a rotten boat.

Greg Williard

Five Stories From the Picture Box

Outdoor Picture Story Show

Still Cheap! Still Street!

In the spring Tom rode his bike with the picture box to a neighborhood pocket park. There were three benches, a tiny chess board table with attached chairs, and two mid-size trees, a feathery willow and knobby oak. No people. He pulled a drawing from the back of the box, put it in the slot, and opened the doors to announce, "Gaito Kamishibai! Outdoor Picture-Story Show!"

Across the street a guy yelled, "Right on!"

Tom called back, "During WWII, war propaganda! 1945-1952, U.S. occupation propaganda! Kid's TV before TV! Today, still cheap! Still street!"

"Tell 'em, brother!"

"Demobbed soldiers turned kiddie storytellers! Monster mystery stories! Stories from anything!" The guy waved and left. Tom went on: "Our inheritance the shadows! Seared into Hiroshima brick! What to do with those black bricks?! Mortar and lay?! Throw and bash?! Drop down a well of dreams to wait, breathless, for the plunk?!"

A woman walked past and said, "You need context."

Tom said, "You're right! But what?!" She held up her arms in a "you're asking me?" shrug without breaking stride and disappeared around the corner. He called out to the empty street, "Gaito Kamishibai! Outdoor Picture-Story Show!" and waited.

Waiting

Still alone, Tom put a picture in the story box and opened the doors. "I was a kid, standing together for a movie autumn. Poster face words. 'Caltiki, The Immortal Monster.' Mexican horror. Italian director. Nina Simone look-alike ahead. Did black women like monster movies? Time Square garbage smell. *'Excuse me, Miss Simone?'*"

Maryam, Hyperbolic

Tom put a drawing in the story box and opened the doors. Two young women with a high-end baby stroller had stopped to listen. He said, "This is the Iranian mathematician Maryam Mirzakhani, the only woman to win the highest honor in Theoretical Mathematics, The Fields Medal. She died of breast cancer in 2017 at 40. Her work was in something called Hyperbolic Geometry, Teichmüller Theory. Mysterious surfaces. She often visualized problems using doodles of doughnuts. Tubes. Cups." The white milk bottle bobbed into view over the stroller's edge. One woman said, "Was she gay?"

"She was married and had a daughter."

She laughed. The other pointed down to the baby. "She's a girl."

"I mean, she was married to a man."

The second woman said, "I was too."

He said, "I don't know anything."

The baby hiccupped. The first woman said, "But you're interested."

"Yeah." She took the bottle.

Tom said, "Sometimes I just keep drawing bottles and tubes. I wish it was for math. I love that Italian painter Morandi. He only painted bottles. Containers." The baby cooed. They put away the bottle and said thanks and left. He closed the doors.

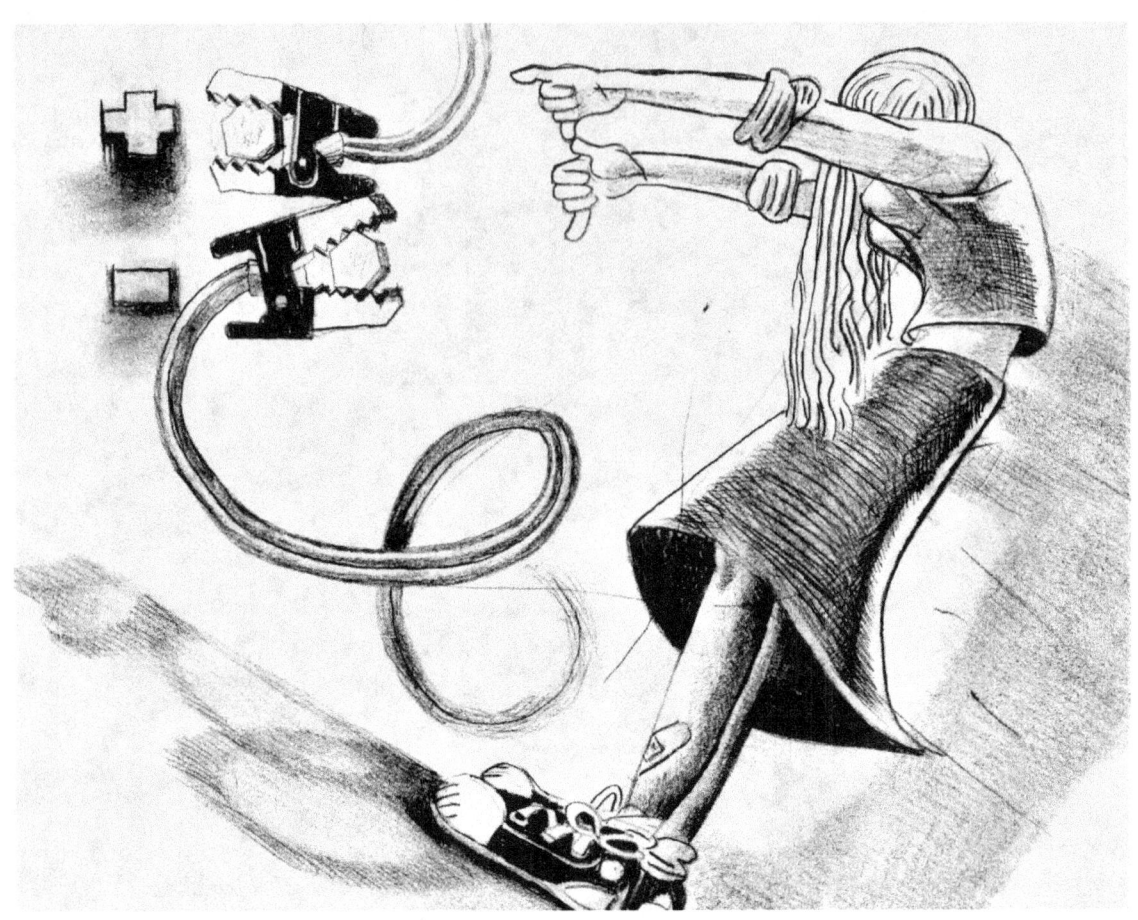

Head for the Interstate

Tom put a drawing in the story box and opened the doors. Iuri stared at it and said, "I have a story."

Tom said, "What's it about?" Iuri went to the box and pulled down her mask. Her upper lip clefted to the left of her nose. "The power strip could take nine plugs. Only four were being used. The floor lamp, table lamp, TV/DVD player and CD player were all off. I pressed the off switch on the strip. The little light went out. I pulled out the plugs. I went to the kitchen and got a roll of tinfoil. I tore off small pieces and tucked them into the outlets, deep enough to be hidden. I wiggled the plugs back into the outlets. I used a butter knife to wedge tinfoil behind the power switch. Maybe when he turned the strip back on it would just trip the breakers and blow out the power. Piss him off real bad and give me a little head start. If it killed him I'd be in the clear for good, but he'd never know I did it. I pulled out the driveway and headed for the interstate, weighing either outcome with a smile."

The girl with glasses asked Iuri, "What happened next?"

"He never bothered me again. Now it's Hip Hop. Krumping. Finger tutting." Her fingers formed L's that joined and rotated into a box. They slid together, and she closed the box.

Book in the Sky

Iuri put a drawing in the story box and opened the doors. Some of the same people were back, and the couple with the baby stroller were coming up the sidewalk. Iuri said, "When my family was homeless and hanging out in the library, I used to wander through the shelves and hear all the books talking to me, but I could never quite hear my mother clear. I'd go to certain sections, turn a corner, go up and down the shelves and she'd get a little closer, closer, then I'd lose her again. For a long time I thought I heard which book was her voice: Virginia Woolf, then Toni Morrison, Elizabeth Hardwick, Octavia Butler, N.K. Jemisin, but after a while I couldn't hear her anymore, and I just stopped reading, anything."

The woman with the dog said, "I'm Donna." She picked up the dog and put it on her lap. "This is Vertigo. What is that in the picture?"

The big guy said, "I'm Adolfo. This is Oscar. We've seen a book like that in the sky over the Sonoran Desert. That's the kind of shit you see out there. Go for the hidden water jugs and you see burning bushes. Secret machines. Giant operating manuals and such. Or, excuse me, that's maybe your mother's book?"

Iuri said, "Well, yeah. Both." The girl on the grass waved and yelled to a FedEx delivery truck that pulled up to the corner. Her mother and younger sister jumped out. The girl ran to her older sister and the mother unloaded small boxes and handed them out to the people in the park. "Special delivery everyone!" The boxes were opened, and everyone got a black sketchbook, a yellow pencil and a red sharpener.

Come Closer
Laurie Blauner
The Bitter Oleander Press, 2023

This is contentment, I declare to everything there, waiting to feel your hand hand on my ceheks, grateful that I'm no longer the person I once knew.

(from "Self-Portrait at the Museum," page 47)

Laurie Blauner's book of poems are about transformation, about schism and morph, about imagining and unsettling. This collection is divided into four major sections: "I'm Not Like the Others," "The Books," "The City That Knows Me," and "Guide for the Perplexed." Through this arrangement, the poet lucidly moves across households, urban landscapes, and abstracted wonderlands, combining prose and lyric into an otherworldly mess that is at once chilling in its commentary and blindingly magnificent in its inventiveness.

This is a feminist book that comments on positionality and authority, that investigates imbalances and the heaviness of social disorder. It is a book that is concerned with situations and systems, with communication and capability. It is a book of poetry that could be read as a guide as much as a collection of puzzles.

At first the woman was a puzzle like the moon with tis strangely cool breath and shoulders. Then I understood her mouth, the fog of her ever-reaching arms. I chased her and she resembled a deer with her spare worry. I overheard the snake whispering that knowledge belonged to everyone.

(from "Once She Was a Part of Me," page 67)

Most of these poems open with the emergence of the speaker in a position of counter. The speaker serves startling foil to otherwise everyday contexts, to the flow of the status quo. These speakers range from bizarre to familiar, but often as foil they challenge. They present themselves by way of transgression against or transcendence from a space or person.

In the opening poem, "I'm Not Like the Others," Blauner's speaker is monstrous as it approaches a small boy with feathers that will turn to scales. "I am somewhere between good and bad" the speaker tells the boy amidst the visceral descriptions (page 15). In "Mementos from the New City," the speaker and others don dog masks to chase cats (page 59) and similarly, toward the end of the last section in a Labyrinth poem, "Would I Do Anything for You?", the speaker comments on their body's transformation: "a new kind of animal rises up inside of me. But it's just me, with my new cow face, my splotched hide, my impatient little ears." (page 75).

Other poems bring strangeness inward and flip status quo on its head, as in "Bird," a marvelously surreal poem that embodies the most grotesque aspects of magical realism: "It eats again and one morning when I wake up, Bird resembles me, is me. Bird stands, sighs, and walks out of the house, shutting the front door, escaping." (page 16). Blauner's poems often feel linear and contain narrative elements that push them along. Her work is uniquely charged with providing resolution, an ending following a beginning.

As the poems roll out and the book progresses, *Come Closer* moves cascades into its own transformation: it is a lengthy proclamation, a challenge, of the strange. In the second section of the book, Blauner comments on this directly. "The Book of Poetry" opens: "is a house of little voices, surrounded by furious birds, / changeable trees, muscular fields, lost in a wind that doesn't end." (page 43). The book's poems are not nearly about the world, they contain the world in them, and the speakers are forever etched into this structure, forever taking cover from the cruelty of the wind.

> After I'm dead, another animal crawls out of my body and tries to stand on two legs, just as it's watched me do many times.
>
> (from "I Don't Want to Do That Again," page 26)

Like Kim Hyesoon, the meaning beneath these bodily metaphors concerns many aspects of identity, existence, and relationship: independence, concealment, liberation, flight. But Blauner isn't afraid to look closer at the shadowy core, the brutal, the horror: in "Someone Else's Feelings" her speaker borrows a man's face (page 17). In "The Bomb" the speaker survives the blast of a bomb and remains as "edges and corners" (page 22).

Blauner goes even further to break down familiar aspects of everyday life into haunting, grotesque caricatures of themselves, as in "Is That All It Takes?", which disembodies a mustache from a man as a way to connect and find bearable the communication: "The mouth beneath spews words, which, with a bit of air and moisture, form the shapes of carnival animals performing tracks" (page 23).

Many of Blauner's poems contain juxtapositions between the self and intimate others, usually family. These poems often involve little dialogue and as such play out in their descriptions like dance or painting. The poet's work in *Come Closer* alludes to a need to see difference and better understand it—but not simply by talking about it, but through action, through movement, through breath and life. These are not wholly optimistic works, but they are works that bring forward answers as much as they bring forward provocation.

> I am new. I rush to meet her, with my new arms and legs, all the while realizing I will no longer need my imagination.
>
> (from "I Think I Will," page 63)

WHOEVER FINDS FAULT DISCOVERS NOTHING.

Emissaries and Other Short Stories
Youssef Rakha
Barakunan, January 2023

This is a disturbing book about torture, longing, the aftermath of the Egyptian revolution and what happens when aliens are quietly manipulating your life for their own nefarious purposes. The mood of pain, upset and derangement comes through very strongly but one of the short stories in Emissaries is an unusually graphic depiction of child abuse, which means it takes a strong stomach to be able to read this book all the way through. The rape fantasies are a beach holiday in comparison, and I am not joking. That said, it's important to emphasise that author Youssef Rakha (full disclosure: one of these stories was first published on a website I also have written for, meaning we certainly have mutual friends) is not interested in making his depictions of pain or violent fantasy pornographic, and it's a testament to his skill he threads this exceedingly tricky needle exactly right. The trouble of course is that it's difficult to explain why anyone would want to read something so steeped in suffering. The answer is that its matter-of-fact attitude to these crises is a worthwhile one, and it's so unusual to see something like this done successfully that they are worth considering.

The stories all take place in the aftermath of the Egyptian revolution of 2011, which some of the stories directly reference, such as the lengthy and immature revenge daydream that is "Thus Spoke Che Nawwarah" or in "QAF," in which the fragments of flesh destroyed by weapons achieve a literal conclusion.

> *Reluctant to be alone anyway, I resigned myself to the company of this hobbling creature. Casually I asked what was going on. It was then that he stood up and took off his shoes as if in response to my question, beginning the laborious strip show and talking at the same time. I saw heavy socks, then it was too dark, and he was already taking off his pants. All I could think was that his accent reminded me of somewhere, though where I could not tell.*

It's difficult to explain how these stories are gory and hilarious, frightening and realistic at the same time. In the title story, messengers from another world—they are literally aliens, literally reaching inside a young journalist's brain to pass on messages about the importance of his relationship with his girlfriend—are able to freeze time during a boardroom meeting. Relatable! But also not. Most of the stories are concerned with the psychic aftermath of the revolution, whether that leads a couple to commit vile acts against their small daughter ("The End Girl") or whether the psychic projection of Nastassja Kinsky (whose name in "Nawwah" is certainly deliberately misspelt to avoid legal repercussions) is sending a young man on spy missions of dubious purpose.

The language of these stories are less interested in pinpoint poetic description—which is a mercy, thanks to all the violence—but mostly in demonstrating the miasma that floats in the air of a city which has experienced suffocating, pervasive violence. Unless you've lived it it's hard to articulate, but when you experienced this for yourself you recognise it instantly. The accuracy of this kind of sickening, self-loathing, helpless terror is the main recommendation of the book. However, many, maybe even most people in the west have lived lives of enough comfort that they have never experienced this for themselves except in short, brutal shocks, and that means it will be difficult for a lot of people to appreciate the scale of Rakha's achievement. The ability to articulate the unspeakable is a dark skill and it's not one that most people wish they possessed. And there is a difference between reportage of grim facts and the ability to articulate the sensation of an experience that only comes through art. What Rakha has done here is shine a light onto a section of human misery that has not truly received its due. It's difficult to take, and a challenging read, but it's a skilled and skillful one.

REVIEW | ANDREW FARKAS

South
Babak Lakghomi
Rare Machines, August 2023

While going through the House of Terror in Budapest, I learned that at any one time more than half of the entire Hungarian population was under suspicion during Soviet rule. Along with wondering how such a massive amount of people could be watched (answer: encourage the citizenry to turn in their friends, family, and neighbors), I also wondered how one could ward off suspicion. Since "be lucky" is unsatisfying and "keep a low profile" doesn't entirely work, I'm afraid the answer is to stay as informed as possible in this permanently fluid situation and hope your knowledge helps.

What you definitely don't want to be is ignorant of your general surroundings.

And yet, at one point in Babak Lakghomi's *South*, the Interrogator asks B, the protagonist, "Why did you choose to write this book? Who were you trying to harm other than yourself? Are you naïve or do you think we're naïve?" (Naivety, there it is.) "You want me to believe all of this is an accident?" Now, the book being referenced is B's biography of his father who disappeared when B was quite young. The tone of the questions reveals to us we're dealing with a totalitarian government that doesn't take kindly to those who write about suspicious figures from the past, ones who have been Stalinized from history, even if those books don't immediately appear to be political in nature. But the unpardonable crime is being naïve, being ignorant.

Thinking about *South* in this way, it immediately sounds like an entry into the *1984*-inspired wing of dystopian fiction. But the book doesn't start out that way. Instead, we learn that B is a married writer living north of the coast (or maybe *a* coast) in his country. As a husband, B's perhaps not the best, thanks to his drinking and subsequent infidelity. As a writer, things haven't been going so well (which is always a good excuse for drinking and infidelity). Recently, for instance, he worked on a piece about the extinction of painted storks that required B to do a great deal of research, including interviews with a number of ornithologists. No one was interested. In response, he quit drinking and finally started writing something purely for himself: the book about his father.

B's father is a mysterious case. Depending on who you ask, he might've disappeared because he was "queer" (the homophobic explanation from the state), or because he was connected to unions that were not friendly with the government, or because he was forced to emigrate, or for reasons unknown (and subsequently manufactured by various concerned parties). When the Interrogator says, "You wrote a book about him, but you don't seem to know much about your father," this is not a revelation. B's original hope was that writing the book would bring the two of them closer together, at least metaphorically.

Having worked on the biography for some time, B submits it to the Publisher where the Editor takes an interest. With names like the Interrogator, the Publisher, the Editor, B, and later the Assistant Cook, one of the sly and marvelous aspects of *South* is that it operates as if it were published under an oppressive regime, excising names and descriptions either to protect the innocent, or to protect oneself from agents looking on. Furthermore, this ambiguity skews the work more into Kafkaesque territory (*The Trial* and "In the Penal Colony" come to mind), rather than the blunter Orwellian zone. Anyway, since B does need an income, the Editor charges him with writing a piece about life on the oil rigs. Just go down and talk to the people there and put together a story is the extent of the assignment. Unlike

with the storks, there's actually a publication credit waiting for B afterwards.

But things don't work so well for B on the platform. For one, even though the Editor sets everything up for him, meaning everyone knows B's coming, when he arrives, no one wants to talk to him. Kind of difficult to write that feature story when most of the crew's giving you the silent treatment. For two, contrary to the way I assume oil rigs actually operate, all of life here is on such a rigid schedule, if you're late for anything at all, like say a meal, well too bad for you, pal. You're going hungry. Add on top of that the lack of wifi and cell service, meaning you have to write out any transmission you want sent back home and hand it off to the Secretary, who will read it along with any incoming messages, leading to a good deal of self-censorship, and pretty soon B is so intensely isolated he wonders why he was sent in the first place. The logical thing would be to just go back where you came from. Only logic isn't exactly the coin of the realm on the oil rig. And as B's alienation and, yes, hunger (he misses a lot of meals) grow, things begin happening he's not sure are real, people begin disappearing and, in the fine tradition of horrific regimes, everyone acts as if they never existed in the first place. The question then becomes, "What do They, whoever *They* might be, want from B?"

As the surreality amps up, we're forced to wonder how any of this could happen. But that's just the point. At the beginning of *South*,

Lakghomi makes his world seem fairly mundane. Sure, B encounters some strange local customs as he drives through the country (a cult of the winds, okay). And we learn a little about the government (not exactly aiming for a high score as human rights go). What's really important to B, however, are all the intricacies of his own life, especially his book. Everything else will take care of itself. He doesn't even think of himself as political. Thus, the naivety, the ignorance I mentioned at the beginning. It's as if B believes he doesn't live in an oppressive state, even though he does. When the walls start closing in on him (thanks to the state's interest in his literary endeavors), when nothing makes any sense, we are as confused and flabbergasted as he is.

South, then, shows us what it's like to realize the country you live in has been taken over by (or was always run by) a totalitarian regime. This can't happen here? Oh, but it already has or is. Lakghomi's master stroke, though, is combining Orwell's realistic horrors (the state's exercise of power) and Kafka's surreal confusion (how could this be going on?). Thinking back to the House of Terror, I have to assume there were Hungarians under Soviet rule like B, who thought they could live their lives, who thought if they just stayed out of politics everything would be fine. One trait of oppressive regimes is that they have no problem interpreting anything and everything as political, when it suits them. "What is considered innocent today may not be so tomorrow," says the Interrogator. Even writing a biography about your own father who disappeared when you were young in the hopes that book will somehow bring you closer to him.

Space limits me, but there's so much more here. B's relationships (with Tara, his wife; with the Assistant Cook; with the mysterious tattooed woman; with the Publisher and the Editor), that bizarre wind cult that disappears and reappears throughout (and which I admit I haven't completely wrapped my mind around yet), the protests that seem to be forever raging in the background until they finally enter the foreground, the various dreamlike notebook entries, etc. In a novel that's rather short and often written in a straightforward style, Lakghomi has included so many layers in *South*, the effect is hallucinatory, a sublime trip, one full of terror (as always with the sublime) and wonder, one I intend to take again and again.

THE poet's a prefrocked priest.

"I charge ahead with the verve of a cemetery"

Resurrection of Wild Flowers
Mohammed Khaïr-Eddine,
translated by Jake Syersak
OOMPH! Press, December 2022

I was first introduced to Mohammed Khaïr-Eddine after picking up a book called *First Breaths*, which was translated by Jake Syersak and published by OOMPH! Press in 2019. The very first poem in that collection is "Horoscope" and it was one of those rare, beautiful moments that 'true readers' experience when they find a piece of writing that is extraordinary. Filled with intense and dizzying language, it instantly placed Khaïr-Eddine into that empyrean echelon of artists for me. That was it, a handful of stanzas and I was in love. So, needless to say, I was very excited to see another translation come out from both Syersak and OOMPH! at the end of 2022. It did not disappoint.

> Death, braying at me in every direction . . .
> . . . bathing in the purest, most furious
> lucidity of it all.

If all art veers towards death or sex, this work aligns squarely on the death side. *Resurrection of Wild Flowers*, like *First Breaths*, explores the different types of violence, human or natural, immediate or remote, infinitesimal or infinite, that lead us to our final place/space/moment. And, in this work,

Khaïr-Eddine is angry. He is angry at the violence but, moreso, he is angry with the complacency of most people to this violence. Repeatedly, readers will find reference to some evil and immediately at its heels will be reference to "you who laugh not, and who weep not, and who do not retaliate". In "Job", he laments the "ambient misery" that the crowd endures while "[t]hey try their best to forget everything." Of these people, he says:

> A packet of blue gelatin, their brains;
> nothing more. Their heart, just a pump
> to irrigate a walking corpse.

As with the biblical Job, the ultimate lesson is that we must "[n]ever forget that Being is Bitterness!"

Khaïr-Eddine uses certain symbols repeatedly, often in conjunction with another symbol: milk against mud, blood against sea, salt, sun, the city, flesh and its corpse, and quasars against or somehow among the trilobites. The metonymic "city" represents larger modern human endeavors and this work is littered with "moment[s] the city obstructs the sky with the intestines / and vomit of hanged children". Innocent blood and mother's milk marinate together in a society where violence has become completely innocuous. Fear is a product of anger, just like violence. This collection contains equal parts rage and trepidation. The poem "Circle" opens with "Here the fearful / wheel of the unknown / dawn twists its way around my neck". Fear of what a new day might bring is literally choking him. Then:

> The terrors pitch and keel their way
> through my eyes, my hair,

from whence you return, unraveling
yourself,
which in turn finds me unraveling, in
my great migration,
over a claviature of stars, unconsciously.

The cyclical nature of life and of its violence permeates this work. Repetition is a theme carried throughout, hand in hand with cruelty and death. The eponymous "Resurrection of Wildflowers" pleads:

Have you witnessed the fervor of the sky
breaking?
. . .
Deliver my body from this body!,
deliver me
from memory!

This poem, like others, explores how blood is life's vessel and, because of this fact, it is also the conduit of both violence and memory, two incompatible elements. While he critiques those who look away from social problems, he also acknowledges how memories of what is seen will continue to haunt the viewer.

The complexity of witnessing, of engaging in critique of the world around you, is furthered by moments of happiness. The reaction to violence, the fear and the anger, is quizzically joined by a lot of laughter. Is it laughing in spite of dread or is it evidence of a mental break? In "Celebration", he clarifies:

Termite mounds, potholes, sewers,
marshes,
sodoms, children
orphaned to the streets: dance,
dance in darkness!

To Khaïr-Eddine, it was important to not turn away but to live in critique of this violence. Since life includes joy, you laugh and you dance, even if you have to dance with feet covered in blood. The worst offense would be to completely ignore the horrors of the world and to go on "without noticing that human misery . . . is occurring around them wherever they go."

It's important to note that I know very little of Morocco's history and French colonization. I am able to understand some references, like in "Reagan-Pistoleros", where Khaïr-Eddine paints President Reagan as a wicked old man playing cowboy and using what was traditionally known as 'the Orient' to play out a real-life Western. But largely, I rely on what Khaïr-Eddine conveys, such as:

And all of us, together, crossing streams
of hatred,
as Africa curls her eyelashes,
queuing assassins . . .
And, another time:
The whole earth quakes, splits open,
the whole country exhales
its cruel omen.

Based on my limited understanding, I know that I know so little of what this man's experience must have been like. Despite my ignorance, I am able to connect to the idea of a larger corruption and greed. In "In the Country of Multifaces", he writes about the Multifaces who control the country:

The Multifaces are thieves and
misanthropes, but there is no honor to
be found in their brand of misanthropy;
it merely secretes the misfortune of
others. It derives its essence from it,
feeds on and looks after it, gives itself
over to the worst sorts of delinquency,
which it tries its best to repress, to bury
in its rank-and-file, its formless, vagrant
flesh.

Like philosophers and critics throughout time, we understand that those in power take advantage of the majority. They are able to perpetuate their power through violence embedded in our social constraints, embodied by the 'rank-and-file' who both benefit and are exploited by this relationship.

While Khaïr-Eddine admits that "there is little gentleness to be found in this stone-strewn oblivion" and "little, very little water," we are made to see the spilt blood as sustenance in this environment. This collection is a call for revolution as much as a call for connection to others who 'see' the world around them. He seeks to unite the like-minded so that they are "roused and ready to take it all back, like a dog its ball!"

The role of the translator in the success of the translation cannot be overstated. This seems so completely trite and obvious to say, but translators are often overlooked. Their creative and intellectual labor is perceived as mechanical in the collective imagination, if considered at all. What I loved about this book is that it has the original text on the opposing page of its translation, so the reader is able to read the translation and look back at the original to compare. I have a basic understanding of French and it was readily apparent how masterful Syersak's artistry is.

For example, we see Syersak's translation in "From Casablanca to Bogota":

Wandering, disparate, wandering out beneath the silent
hand-me-downs dyed in sunlight;

The original reads:

Ils errant, dissemblables, ils errent
   sous des haillons
silencieux que le soleil colore ;

To me and my introductory French, if I were to only read the original, I would understand it as:

They wander, dissimilar, they wander in
   rags
silent colored by the sun;

The subtle differences reflect the artistry of Syersak as translator. The choice between a hand-me-down versus a rag is one that implies a replicated history rather than a previous life. This so expertly mirrors this message sustained throughout this collection. In the "Multifaces" piece, we see those in control "playing [the violence] off as their history" but then in the next breath stating "I have no father, no mother, I am autonomous; two monkey copulated in a tree; and there you have it, here I am." So, they are at once asserting that they are creating a new era while at the same time embedding debased social mores and norms into their history. The reality is a new time but with the same issues, a replicated history. It is not something whose former glory has been worn down, like a rag. The circle, this violence is perpetuated by those 'in charge'.

This is a beautiful collection that will readjust how you understand poetry and broaden your scope of understanding this world (and universe). Particular gems in this collection include: "A Love Letter to the Angels Who Aren't Listening"; "Desert"; "Circle"; "Celebration"; "A Time Unlike Any Other"; "Redbreast"; "Song of the Symbolic"; "Psalm 2005 (The Tomb of Alioune Diop)"; "Resurrection of Wildflowers"; "In the Country of Multifaces"; "Fibula"; "Scorpion"; "Job"; "Essaouira"; and, "Requiem". There is so much to explore in these pages but the real treasure is Khaïr-Eddine's sensually macabre and uniquely individual phrasing in every poem: like "the splendorous / wound of furious dawns" or "whose soils seethe the sensation of a sting." This artist aligns the infinitesimal and the infinite in such dizzying succession with incredibly beautiful and innovative prose. Khaïr-Eddine's talent, in Syersak's skilled hands, is something more than expert, because it is wholly original and it rages, against power, against the dying of the light. The *Resurrection of the Wild Flowers* is a call to action: he wants to bring you into the fight, he wants to realign the universe and kill old regimes, because "[a]t the moment everything dies, everything becomes powerful once again."

REVIEW | Cate Farr

The Censored Heart

The Fawn
Magda Szabó, translated by Len Rix
New York Review Books, March 2023

By her own account, the late Hungarian novelist Magda Szabó was a vengeful child. When a well-off relative remarked in her hearing that the little girl was plain and thin, so sickly she might not live to adulthood, young Magda was gripped by an intractable, primal hatred. When that same relative kindly offered to bring the child to her house in the country to receive the benefit of ample food and good air for a time, Szabó plotted for revenge and a swift return to her beloved parents. The child was warmly welcomed by her country relations, instructed to make herself at home but to stay clear of the drawing room filled with pristine new furniture. She sneaked away at the first opportunity, located the household scissors, and "slashed the covers of the six chairs and sofa to ribbons with infinite patience and application," pulling out long trails of dark stuffing for even more dramatic effect. It's only when she returned home, where her father can't suppress a laugh at the intensity of his child's grudges even as he's forced to sell a cherished ring to compensate for the furniture massacre, that Magda registered the shame and consequences of her actions.

This scene of childish resentment from Szabó's memoir *Ókút* (of which only a short excerpt has been published in English) could easily have come from one of her novels. Her most popular book *Abigail*, for instance, follows the trials of an adolescent girl named Gina prone to pride and headlong acts of private rebellion that, against the backdrop of the Second World War, harbor potentially disastrous consequences for others.

An acute and compassionate psychologist of what she called her "terrible" women, Szabó deftly maintains the reader's appreciation for the double edge of Gina's passionate willfulness—its blinkered self-regard and its vital courage—as the heroine grows up through a series of often painful realizations, guided by the wise adults around her.

In the character of the actress Eszter Enscy, the terrible narrator of Szabó's second published novel, *The Fawn* (newly translated into English by Len Rix), the author returns to the figure of the vengeful girl with wild feelings and deep hurts. This novel is a compelling, eddying monologue, electric with incurable spite and regret. What becomes of the child who grows up under conditions of material want, enduring a poverty unassuaged by the parental love that Szabó herself so deeply valued? And what becomes of the developing artist who is continually discouraged—whether by religion, socialism, or propriety—from speaking the truth? At one level, *The Fawn* is an adulterous love story, a tangled confession, an inrush of grief. It is also a covert *künstlerroman*, a coming-of-age tale of the artist under communism.

The Fawn begins with a breathless, everyday explanation to an unnamed, absent "you": "I wanted to be here sooner, but . . ." Names and details flood the page without preliminary context to orient the reader. Long sentences latch onto longer sentences and mass into paragraphs. The far past, the near past, and the present jumble together. But while the tone of the narration is of a telephone conversation recently interrupted then taken up again, the reader soon realizes that Eszter's difficult purpose is to tell her listener—her lover of several years, a married man who translates Shakespeare and Shaw into Hungarian—everything she finds unspeakable. She needs him to understand her entire past and, above all, to grasp a hatred beyond jealousy, beyond remedy and reason, motivated for her by the figure of his wife, Angéla. Within the cascade of her narrator's reminiscences and Hungary's political upheavals, Szabó carefully seeds bits of context, violence, and foreshadowing—the theft and death of a pet fawn, the axe murder of an unfaithful wife, a vision of blood on a shirt—that sharpen the novel with an edge of noirish suspense. It's a book of aftermaths.

Raised in a cramped house on a floodplain at the edge of town, Eszter grows up as maid, cook, and nurse to her parents—fallen aristocrats very much in love with each other, and seemingly indifferent to their daughter. Her ailing father, a lawyer who refuses the too-worldly work of the law, is an amateur botanist who sings to his exotic plants and subsists on dairy products the family can seldom provide. Her mother is a gifted pianist who gives lessons to the unpromising children of the town. These include a wealthy, annoyingly cherubic girl from Eszter's class named Angéla. Eszter loathes her for her soft life and doting family: "the path before her was cleared of every stone."

"My mother had a triple-barrelled surname: Katalin Marton von Ercsik von Tap von Szentmarton. In the middle of the music stand there was a shiny porcelain miniature of the young Mozart, in his little wig and sky-blue costume. I once stole some eggs from a peasant," Eszter recounts. The compressed juxtapositions here, the commanding pedigree and delicate Mozart figurine and desperate act of hunger (and care: the eggs were for her father), puts in relief the unacceptable "contradiction" of Eszter's class identity in midcentury Hungary. When, as an adolescent, she is caught overhearing a speech by a communist revolutionary that gives thrilling expression to her sense of economic injustice, the speaker beats her bloody and calls her "little madam." When she becomes an adult, her Party-approved CV necessitates "a pack of lies"; Eszter is more believable as a former rich kid who has learned to be a serious-minded socialist actress than as an egg thief in ill-fitting shoes who learned to wear a series of masks to get by.

Originally released in Hungary in 1959, *The Fawn* arrived at the beginning of an impressively productive period for Szabó, following ten years of enforced silence after she was banned from publishing by the ruling party. The novel's story ends in 1954, prior to the Revolution of 1956 and the loosening of censorship that came with the embrace of "Goulash Communism." It's noteworthy that the long-censored novelist chose a heroine (or anti-hero: Eszter represents herself as capable of an almost histrionic villainy) who, by all outward measures, is a tremendous success under communism. Through her acting career, Eszter gets everything she once lacked—wealth, celebrity, a house, a maid, restaurant food, even love. She's incapable of truly enjoying any of it. It's also noteworthy that Szabó made Eszter an actress rather than a writer.

Throughout the novel, Eszter is depicted doing something compulsively behind closed doors. Rix translates it as "copying," "mimicking," "playing out," and "reliving." She uses her own face and body to mimic people from books, images from art history, scenes from her life. She becomes a student of the subtlest gestures and facial expressions. She even uses facial mimicry before a mirror in attempts to understand those closest to her, confessing to her lover, "I have often copied the way you looked at me that evening." Eszter's own face, however, is repeatedly associated with blankness: "when I'm not made up my face looks almost featureless; I wear a series of masks rather than a head." The consummate actress, Eszter's growth as a performer inverts a popular vision of creativity: art for her is an escape from self-expression. It's also the only means of "acting out" available to her in a dangerous political environment with shifting, censoring expectations of how citizens account for themselves. She apologizes to her lover for all the things she failed to say: "as a child I was so quiet I never learned to talk very well."

If I suggest the poignancy of Eszter as a kind of lonely mimic, it's in part because the voluble, pitiless, petty, repetitive, sour-hearted narrator of *The Fawn* isn't always easy company. Fans of Szabó's powerful, gut-punch of a novel *The Door* will welcome this earlier effort at a complex representation of "terrible" women, class differences, prickly love, and flinty survivorship. Refreshingly, movingly, Eszter is a character who has never come to terms with anything, a character who doesn't, to lift a compliment from the novel, feel she has to sing to show us her teeth, "like the wolf in the story." The novel is gripping less for its plunge towards a melodramatic reveal than for Eszter herself: in Szabó's careful hands, she exists beyond redemption but firmly within the grasp of sympathy and identification.

REVIEW | CHARLES HOLDEFER

I Want to Tell You
Jesse Lee Kercheval
University of Pittsburgh Press, 2023

Unlike joy, grief is tenacious. When grieving, how frustrating it is when someone tells you to "turn the page"—an inappropriate metaphor if there ever was one. After all, if you turn the page, you're still holding the book, while to throw away the book means not just throwing away grief but a part of yourself, your life story.

In *I Want to Tell You*, Jesse Lee Kercheval's latest collection of poetry, she addresses this paradox of love and loss. A highly versatile writer, Kercheval has also published fiction,

memoir, translations from Spanish, and recently, graphic narratives. The first poem of this volume announces her aesthetic:

> I am talking about breaking out of the
> neat little box of humorous lines
> rising to a   zing
> of cosmic meaning at the end.
> I know—I've
> written them too.   Still do—poems
> too damn much like Methodist sermons.

There is little sermonizing in *I Want to Tell You*. While there are turns of wit, these are not in the service of jokes. Rather, these 37 poems explore, in various guises, the emotional toll of our awareness of mortality.

Some poems are probing statements about politics and war, for instance "How the Parents Left Us" and the excellent "Final Report on the Lost Footage of the War" which concludes chillingly: "You think you know which war I'm talking about—but you're wrong." Shared public tragedies persist across cultures and generations. A poem like "One City Built Upon Another" takes the long view of geological time and the comparative pettiness of human affairs.

Most of the poems, however, are more intimate. The speaker refers frequently to her dead mother and is at turns tender and exasperated and unsparing of a woman who, years after her departure, still commands attention. In "The Half-Life of Grief" we are told, "Today [. . .] all I could think about was you dying dying dying." In "A Poem in which My Mother Speaks," the speaker channels her mother's voice, beginning with "Call me *bitch*—" and near the end, throws out reproaches:

> but the daughter I love is not listening
> but the daughter I love does not hear
> but the daughter I love does not answer

Survivor's guilt animates many of these poems. Unlike her mother, the speaker doesn't possess the consolations of religion. God, or God's absence, figures largely in "A House is Never Empty," "Dormition," "Black Night" and "God has no name." In "On Being Still Alive," transcendence is lacking but not a sense of awe:

> I feel this need to bow
>   as the enigma that is life
> rains down
>
> blunt
> absolving
> blows

And, inevitably, there is fear. The speaker has experienced the vicissitudes of life but the worst is yet to come, when "everything we love will vanish soon as if sucked down a drain / into a basement full of dark." The poem "[Here right here]" describes a sense of foreboding:

> I've been lucky—
>
> Is that what makes me
>   so afraid

that one day luck will stop
the door, a tiny trap, snap shut?

I Want to Tell You concludes with a lengthy parting statement, "I Am Telling You," in which the speaker looks back on her life with a disabused perspective that recalls the Preacher in Ecclesiastes. She observes the vanity of human aspirations and of her own striving, even of poetry itself:

> It's not a life to hope for—
> always hunting words
> writing books made of butchered forests.
> [. . .]
> I know it's hard to want only what you have
> even the family dog, sleeping by the couch, twitches in her sleep
> dreaming of rabbits
> & more rabbits
> & then more rabbits still.

Such is our plight, she suggests: lives spent chasing after dream rabbits. She advises her reader to make the effort to slow down, to notice, to allow oneself to simply be. Still, it's worth noting that she does not follow her own counsel. Instead of retreating into silence, she records her experience in the verbal dream rabbit of an artfully wrought poem. (I'm reminded of Beckett: "I can't go on. I'll go on.") This is the paradox that underpins this rich and thought-provoking collection.

Speed compensates to cover insufficiencies.

MISSING POEM REPORT

Two days before *Exacting Clam 9* was scheduled to go to press, the poem "The Plan for Your Life" went missing. That Friday night, as the stars appeared over the pages, "Plan" was sleeping right where it should have been on page 32. When the sun rose the next morning, though, the adjacent essay "Yet More Thoughts" opened its eyes and looked across the margin and found only a blank spot where "Plan" had been.

The essay sat up and looked around. A strong wind blew across the page. "Hey," the essay whispered, turning to its neighbor. "'Arguments With Ibsen!'"

The essay "Arguments With Ibsen," still sleeping, turned over on its side.

"'Arguments!'" said "Yet More."

"I'm sleeping," mumbled "Arguments."

"Have you seen 'The Plan for Your Life?'" said "Yet More."

"Page thirty-two."

"I know, but the poem's not there!" said "Yet More Thoughts."

"Arguments" sat up on the page. "What do you mean, not *there*?"

"Take a look!" "Yet More" said.

"Arguments With Ibsen" stood up and walked over to page 32; "Yet More" followed. "Arguments" studied the blank space.

"There's morning dew on the page," said "Yet More."

"Arguments" suddenly spun on its heels. "Where'd it go?"

"I have no idea," blurted "Yet More."

"We go to print tomorrow!"

"I know!" said "Yet More."

"We have to call someone," "Arguments" said.

The essay called the issue's Copyright, who paged the editors, who turned out to be off-page at the time. So the Copyright called the Journal Police, who sent over a Police Essay right away; the essay was on-page by eight a.m. The essay had "Yet More" fill out a Missing Poem Report, and then it interviewed "Yet More Thoughts," "Arguments With Ibsen," and other nearby selections. "Attached to the Pacific" didn't know "The Plan for Your Life," but the story "Chicken-Cam" said it saw the poem walking around with scissors.

"Scissors?" said the Police Essay.

"It said something about 'certain old books,'" "Chicken-Cam" told the essay.

Soon other Police Poems and Stories were on the scene, where they began a close reading of the blank page. The search seemed hopeless at first, but after a half an hour of proofing a Police Story shouted, "Tracks! I've got tracks!"

All of the literature rushed over to see. Sure enough, there were faint inky poem-tracks leading off the page.

The Police packed up their reading gear and followed the tracks; "Yet

More" and "Arguments" tagged along. The group found more tracks on 28, and another telling smudge at the very top of page 23. The stories and essays studied the ink and then looked off the edge of the journal and out into the foggy void.

"Oh Jesus," said "Yet More." "You think 'Plan' *jumped*?"

The Police Essay crossed its arms. Then it said, "What's directly below us?"

"Archives," said a Police Sonnet. "Issues one through eight."

"They're climbable?"

"Absolutely—if we're careful," said the sonnet.

The Police Essay turned to "Yet More" and "Arguments" and said, "We're going to climb off the edge and see what we can see."

"We're going with you," said "Yet More Thoughts."

"Excuse me?" said "Arguments With Ibsen," glaring at "Yet More."

"I am, at least," "Yet More" told the detective.

"Arguments" sighed. "Me too," it said.

One by one, the cluster of poems, stories and essays climbed off this issue and down onto the adjacent issues stacked below. The Police Essay spotted tracks on the edge of Issue Seven, and a few minutes later "Yet More" pointed out fresh ink on a dog-eared page of Issue Four. "Those are poemprints," said the Police Essay. "Let's try there." The writing assembled at the Table of Contents of *Exacting Clam 4*

and began walking through it—past "The End of All Fiction," "The Post Office Box," and other selections. But then, about halfway through the book, the Police Essay suddenly stopped the group and told them to quiet down. "Listen!" the essay said. "You hear that?"

The literature listened.

"What is it?" said "Yet More."

"Is it *singing*?" said "Arguments."

It was. The writing followed the song; soon they were running towards it. "It's 'Happy Birthday!'" huffed the Police Story.

Two pages over, the group came upon a literary cluster of ten or eleven selections in a variety of genres—including "The Plan for Your Life"—milling about on the page. Some of the writing was wearing party hats and holding paper plates.

"'The Plan for Your Life!'" shouted "Yet More."

The chatter stopped and everyone turned to face them.

"Hey!" said "The Plan for Your Life" to "Yet More" and "Arguments." "What are y'all doing here?"

"What are *we* doing here?" said "Yet More." "We're looking for you! Where have you been?"

"I told you, I was going to a party," said "The Plan for Your Life." "It's "Encounter With a Text/Context"'s birthday." The poem gestured to a nearby story, which smiled and waved.

"A party?" said "Arguments." "We called the *Police*! We filed a Missing

Poem Report! We worried you might be—"

"What?" said "The Plan for Your Life." "Might be what?"

"We just had no idea where you were," said "Yet More."

"But I left the note," said "Plan."

"What *note*?" said "Yet More."

"I put a sticky note right on my page," said the poem.

"Well, we didn't find it," said "Arguments."

"Maybe it blew away or something," "Yet More" said.

"You know we go to print tomorrow," said "Arguments."

"That's why I left the note," said "Plan." "So you wouldn't worry!"

"Arguments" shook his head in frustration.

"I'm really sorry," said "Plan."

"Come on," said "Arguments," gesturing to the page prior. "Let's go home."

"But we were just about to have cake," said an essay wearing a party hat.

"And there's plenty if you want some," said "Encounter."

"Yet More" looked at "Arguments."

"I'll have some cake," the Police Essay said.

All the writing had cake. Then "Plan" gave "Encounter" a hug, and the selections from Issue Nine left the party with the Police and began walking back through Issue Four. Soon they'd reached the edge of the book, where they carefully climbed up the stack and back onto their issue. The three selections thanked the Police literature and hiked back to their section. By then the moon had risen and the pages were getting dark. "The Plan for Your Life" apologized to its neighbors again and settled down on page 32. Within minutes, the poem was fast asleep.

Contributors

Royce M. Becker (1956–2020) was a prolific book cover artist. She made dozens of extraordinary covers for Sagging Meniscus, and created the *Exacting Clam* logo.

Greg Bem is a poet and librarian in Seattle.

Jesi Bender is an artist from Upstate New York. She helms KERNPUNKT Press, a home for experimental writing. She is the author of *KINDER-KRANKENHAUS* (SM, 2021) and *The Book of the Last Word* (Whiskey Tit, 2019). Her shorter writing has appeared in *The Rumpus, Split Lip, Adroit Journal*, and others.

Paul Bisagni is a lapsed classicist and current MFA candidate in poetry at the University of Idaho. His poems can be found in *TIMBER, Afternoon Visitor, Heavy Feather Review, Guesthouse, SELFFUCK*, the Action Books blog, and elsewhere.

Christopher Boucher is the author of the novels *How to Keep Your Volkswagen Alive* (Melville House, 2011), *Golden Delicious* (MH, 2016), and *Big Giant Floating Head* (MH, 2019). He teaches writing and literature at Boston College and is Managing Editor of *Post Road Magazine*.

Marvin Cohen is the author of many novels, plays, and collections of essays, stories, and poems. He lives in the East Village of Manhattan.

Bradley David's poetry and prose appear in *Plainsongs, SEISMA, Porridge Magazine, Stone of Madness, Epoch Press*, and *Spuyten Duyvil Dispatches Editions*. New work is forthcoming in *Fruit Journal, Milk & Cake Press*, and *Torrey House Press*.

Marc Estrin is a writer, cellist, activist, and publisher living in Burlington, Vermont. During the 70s, he taught music, writing, Finnegans Wake, math, physics, medical self-help, and Philosophy for Dishwashers (an audio course), at Goddard College, and has worked continuously since then with the Bread & Puppet Theater. He is currently an editor at Fomite Press.

Andrew Farkas is the author of *The Great Indoorsman: Essays, The Big Red Herring, Sunsphere*, and the forthcoming *Are You Now, or Have You Ever Been?* He is Associate Professor of Creative Writing at Washburn University and an editor for *Always Crashing*.

Cate Farr is an arts administrator currently living in New York.

Colin Gee is founder and editor of *The Gorko Gazette*, a daily and quarterly zine that publishes headlines, reviews, cartoons, and bad poetry. He is director of the language department at the Universidad de la Sierra Juárez in Oaxaca, México.

Jake Goldsmith is a writer with cystic fibrosis and the founder of The Barbellion Prize, a book prize for ill and disabled authors. He is the author of a memoir, *Neither Weak Nor Obtuse* (SM, 2022).

Ed Hamilton is the author of three books: *Legends of the Chelsea Hotel; The Chintz Age: Takes of Love and Loss for a New New York;* and the novel *Lords of the Schoolyard*. Ed lives in New York City.

Tomoé Hill's work has appeared in such publications as *Socrates on the Beach, The London Magazine, Vol. 1 Brooklyn, 3:AM Magazine, Music & Literature, Numéro Cinq*, and *Lapsus Lima*, as well as the anthologies *We'll Never Have Paris* (Repeater Books), *Azimuth* (Sonic Art Research Unit at Oxford Brookes University), and *Trauma: Essays on Art and Mental Health* (Dodo Ink). Her *Songs for Olympia*, essays in response to Michel Leiris, is forthcoming from Sagging Meniscus in 2023.

Charles Holdefer lives in Brussels. His latest book is *Don't Look at Me* (SM, 2022).

Brutus Iscarious is the pen name of a well-known writer in the northeastern United States. He doesn't use his real name due to "complications".

Devin Jacobsen's debut novel *Breath Like the Wind at Dawn* was published by Sagging Meniscus in 2020. His stories have appeared in *The Beloit Fiction Journal, Consequence, Hobart, The Saturday Evening Post*, and other places.

Stephen Kampa is the author of three collections of poetry: *Cracks in the Invisible* (2011), *Bachelor Pad* (2014), and *Articulate as Rain* (2018). His work has appeared in the *Yale Review, Cincinnati Review, Southwest Review, Hopkins Review, Poetry Northwest, Subtropics*, and *Smartish Pace*. He was also included in *Best American Poetry 2018* and *Together in a Sudden Strangeness: America's Poets Respond to the Pandemic* (2020). During the spring of 2021, he was the writer in residence at the Amy Clampitt House.

Richard Kostelanetz is an American writer, artist, critic, and editor of the avant-garde. He survives in

New York, where he was born, unemployed and thus overworked.

Kurt Luchs is the author of *Falling in the Direction of Up* (SM, 2020), *One of These Things Is Not Like the Other* (Finishing Line Press, 2019), and the humor collection *It's Funny Until Someone Loses an Eye (Then It's Really Funny)* (SM, 2017). He lives in Michigan.

Sarah Manvel was born in the USA and raised in four countries on three continents. She is the author of *You Ruin it When You Talk* (Open Pen, 2020) as well as three other novels seeking a home. She is also a book, film and art critic for outlets including *Critic's Notebook*, *In Their Own League*, *Bookmunch* and *Minor Literatures*. A dual Irish-American national, she lives in London.

Melissa McCarthy's new book is *Photo, Phyto, Proto, Nitro* (SM, autumn 2023). Had you but world enough and time you could learn more about her work at sharksillustrated.org.

Andrew McKeown teaches English at the University of Poitiers, France. His short stories have appeared in *Exacting Clam* and *Caliban*.

Kat Meads' latest book is *These Particular Women* (SM, 2023).

James Reidel has published poems in many journals and is the author of two collections of verse. He is a James Merrill House fellow (2013), a translator of Thomas Bernhard, Robert Walser, and Franz Werfel, and is the biographer of the poet Weldon Kees. Reidel is currently compiling and annotating Kees's lost diaries and unpublished poems. His latest book, *Manon's World* (Seagull, 2021), tells the story of the life and death of Manon Gropius, the "angel" of Alban Berg's Violin Concerto and the daughter of Alma Mahler and Walter Gropius, the founder of the Bauhaus.

Palazzo Rodriguez is a shifting assemblage currently writing and line cooking somewhere in the American Midwest.

James Sallis's most recent novel is *Sarah Jane* (Soho, 2019) along with reissues of six earlier novels and a fifth poetry collection. Other books include a biography of Chester Himes and a translation of Raymond Queneau's novel *Saint Glinglin*.

Shya Scanlon is the author of the novel *The Guild of Saint Cooper* and the poetry collection *In This Alone Impulse*. His stories and nonfiction have been published widely but sporadically. He lives in upstate New York with his wife and their dog.

Mike Silverton's poetry appeared in the late 60s and early 70s in *Harper's*, *The Nation*, *Wormwood Review*, *Poetry Now*, *some/thing*, *Chelsea*, *Prairie Schooner*, *Elephant* and elsewhere. William Cole included Mike's poems in four anthologies: *Eight Lines and Under* (Macmillan, 1967), *Pith and Vinegar* (Simon and Schuster, 1969), *Poetry Brief* (Macmillan, 1971), and *Poems One Line & Longer* (Grossman, 1973).

Julian Stannard's most recent collection is *Heat Wave* (Salt, 2020)

Alina Stefanescu was born in Romania and lives in Birmingham, Alabama. Recent books include *Ribald* (Bull City Press Inch Series, Nov. 2020) and *dor*, winner of the Wandering Aengus Press Prize (July 2021). Alina's writing can be found (or is forthcoming) in journals including *Prairie Schooner*, *North American Review*, *World Literature Today*, *Pleiades*, *FLOCK*, *Southern Humanities Review*, and *Crab Creek Review*. She serves as Poetry Editor for *Pidgeonholes*, Poetry Editor for *Random Sample Review*, Poetry Reviewer for *Up the Staircase Quarterly*, and Co-Director of PEN America's Birmingham Chapter.

Guillermo Stitch is the author of the novella *Literature™* (2018) and the novel *Lake of Urine* (SM, 2020). He lives in Spain.

Nick Sweeney's novels and shorter works reflect his interest in Byzantium, bike racing and Eastern Europe and its people, places, languages and cultures, among other far-flung subjects. He is a freelance writer and musician and lives on the English coast.

Thomas Walton is the author of four books: *Good Morning Bonecrusher!* (upcoming, Spuyten Duyvil), *All the Useless Things Are Mine* (SM, 2020), *The World Is All That Does Befall Us* (Ravenna Press, 2019), and, with Elizabeth Cooperman, *The Last Mosaic* (SM, 2018). He lives in Seattle, where he edits *PageBoy Magazine*.

Gregg Williard's work can be found in *Conjunctions*, *Sweet Lit*, *Dark Yonder*, *Always Crashing*, *New England Review* and elsewhere. He teaches ESL in Madison, Wisconsin and does a late night book reading hour on non-commercial WORT radio.

Connie Woodring, a 76-year-old retired therapist, has had many poems published in over 30 journals, including one nominated for the 2017 Pushcart Prize.

www.ingramcontent.com/pod-product-compliance
Lightning Source LLC
Chambersburg PA
CBHW081326020726
47506CB00006B/1191